Routledge Revivals

Japan To-day

This book, first published in 1904, aimed to provide an overview of the aspects of everyday Japanese life at the beginning of the twentieth century. This book will be of interest to students of history and Asian Studies.

Japan To-day

James A. B. Scherer

First published in 1904
by Kegan Paul, Trench, Trubner & Co.

This edition first published in 2015 by Routledge
4 Park Square, Milton Park, Abingdon, Oxon OX14 4RN
and by Routledge
605 Third Avenue, New York, NY 10017

Routledge is an imprint of the Taylor & Francis Group, an informa business

© 1904 James A. B. Scherer

All rights reserved. No part of this book may be reprinted or reproduced or utilised in any form or by any electronic, mechanical, or other means, now known or hereafter invented, including photocopying and recording, or in any information storage or retrieval system, without permission in writing from the publishers.

Publisher's Note
The publisher has gone to great lengths to ensure the quality of this reprint but points out that some imperfections in the original copies may be apparent.

Disclaimer
The publisher has made every effort to trace copyright holders and welcomes correspondence from those they have been unable to contact.

A Library of Congress record exists under LC control number: 04009638

ISBN 13: 978-1-138-91281-6 (hbk)
ISBN 13: 978-1-315-69175-6 (ebk)
ISBN 13: 978-1-138-91283-0 (pbk)

"Japan To-Day"

From a drawing by a native artist

JAPAN TO-DAY

BY

JAMES A. B. SCHERER, Ph.D.

Formerly Teacher of English in the Government School at Saga,
Japan ; Now President of Newberry College, South
Carolina ; Author of "Four Princes ; or,
The Growth of a Kingdom"

WITH ILLUSTRATIONS

KEGAN PAUL, TRENCH, TRÜBNER & Co. Ltd.
DRYDEN HOUSE, GERRARD STREET, LONDON, W.
1904

TO

THE BRIDE OF YAMAGUCHI

AND

A LITTLE SAGA MAID

BESSIE AND ISABEL

WITH LOVE

CONTENTS

CHAPTER	PAGE
I. THE CYNOSURE	11

    The Hermit becomes a Hero—The Educational Progress of Japan—The Military Progress of Japan and a Comparison with Russia—A View of Japan To-Day.

II. SUNRISE-LAND 27

    The Name of Japan—Sunrise means Beauty: The Beauty of Kamakura, Enōshima, Nikkō—Sunrise means Mystery: Earthquakes, Tidal Waves, and Volcanoes—Sunrise means Light: Civilization and Christianity; or, Manners versus Morals.

III. VIEWS AWHEEL 55

    Tōkyō in the Rain—A Jinrikisha Ramble—The Wheelman's Paradise—Bishop Potter at Nagasaki.

IV. GLIMPSES OF HOME LIFE 83

    In a Japanese Home—The Children—Festivals and Myths—The Women—Christian Wedlock, so-called.

V. THE AWFUL JAPANESE LANGUAGE 117

    What it is Not—Honorifics—Chinese Complications—The Blunders of Beginners—"Why I Study English."

CONTENTS

CHAPTER   PAGE

VI. SERMONS GARNISHED WITH SMILES 143
    The Buddhist at Church—A Sermon on the Chief End of Man—Tales from Japanese Folk-Lore—A Specimen of Oriental Humor—Religions Old and New.

VII. LIFE IN THE SOUTH 175
    The Island of Kyūshū—A Calm Succeeded by a Storm—The Land of the Unknown Fire—A Sketch of Saga—Life in a Japanese School—Side-Lights on "Demoniacal Possession."

VIII. THE PEOPLE OF THE NORTH 201
    The Aborigines of Japan—Ainu Characteristics—King Penri—Strenuous Pastimes—The Spiritual Traditions of a Primitive People.

IX. JAPANESE TRAITS 223
    Topsy-Turvydom—Negative Traits: The Contempt for Time, the Absence of Nerves, Want of Sympathy, and Lack of Confidence—Positive Traits: Frugality, Politeness, and Industry—The Japanese and Chinese contrasted.

X. AN OPENER OF GATES 255
    The Personality of G. F. Verbeck—His Life Story the History of Modern Japan—The Need for Men to Succeed Him.

XI. THE GATES OF ASIA; OR, THE LARGER MEANING OF THE WAR 283
    Palestine and Japan: "The Circuit of the Heavens"—The Vast Importance of Asia and the Present Problem of China—Russia versus Japan: The Political Argument for Missions—Reasons why Japan may Win this War.

ILLUSTRATIONS

	PAGE
"Japan To-Day" .... *Frontispiece*.	
The Great Buddha at Kamakura	16
Land of the Sunrise Beauty	30
Peasants Transplanting Rice	32
Fuji, the Mountain King	34
Mother and Child	48
Japanese Landscape Gardening	60
Rain-Coats made of Straw	62
A Family Journey	70
A Walking Conservatory	72
Typical Country Scene—a Tea Plantation	76
The Mid-day Meal	88
The Empress in Western Dress	94
Japanese Girls and Women	104
A Wedding in Old Japan	112
Good-Night!	114
Buddhist Priests	146
Around the Brazier	162
A Nagasaki Buddhist Temple	168
Boy Acrobats	182
Southern School-girls	192
Ainu Man and Wife	216
Carpenters at Work	226
The Blind Shampooer	236
A Scene near Nagasaki	262
Two Brothers of Old Japan	270
Gates of the Palace at Tōkyō	286
Japan at War	316

I
THE CYNOSURE

¶ The Hermit becomes a Hero—The Educational Progress of Japan—The Military Progress of Japan and a Comparison with Russia—A View of Japan To-Day

JAPAN TO-DAY

I

THE CYNOSURE

It is only a little country, being smaller than the State of California. Only a twelfth of its land is arable,—that is to say, scarcely more than the territory of our own little Maryland. It has a few mines of coal and copper and iron, with less of silver and gold. It lies off the central eastern coast of the vast continent of Asia, a narrow crescent, bent like Diana's bow,—shaped like the rising moon, and named for the Rising Sun,—bending as far as it can towards the west. It is only a little country, filled with forty millions of little brown people, but it is the cynosure of the eyes of all nations. For exactly fifty years has this been true. In 1854 Commodore Perry opened it, a veritable box of curios for the Western world, whose curiosity for its contents has seemed insatiable. In 1894 curiosity deepened into wonder, when this little bow-shaped country

JAPAN TO-DAY

suddenly pierced the rusty mail of China with the swift, sharp arrow of war, and made that dozing giant rub his eyes. In 1904 wonder has become amazement, as Japan has undertaken to celebrate her fiftieth jubilee of enfranchisement among the nations by a doughty wrestling match with the colossal Slav,—a pygmy gone out against a giant.

How can these things be? How has it been possible for a nation apparently to be born in a day, suddenly emerging from sheer Oriental hermitage to become the cynosure of every eye? What accounts for Japan's rapid development from a curio-box to a world-power, so that to-day she is rightly entitled to be called the gate to the Orient? The answer is in one word: Education.

But education predicates two things: advantages and ability. It is of no use to bring opportunity to a man unless he has the grasp which will enable him to seize it by the forelock. Culture will avail him nothing unless he has capacity, just as land must have native fertility before it will respond to cultivation. The mental soil of the Japanese has had a rapid receptivity without parallel in the history of the world.

For five years I taught Japanese students.

THE CYNOSURE

Simply as students, they are ideal. I can see them now, as they sat there, apparently so stoical, so Easternly impassive. But those sleepy-looking eyes were wide awake. Their minds were drinking with a thirst that could never be quenched. And when the next day came, they had digested the lesson of the day before, in every atom, and were clamoring with a hundred questions for more. I do not say that they are an originative race; in a subsequent chapter I shall show that they are not. But I repeat that for quick receptiveness and rapid, thorough assimilation of mental food they are unparalleled.

In the seventh chapter of this volume I shall sketch the actual experiences of an American teacher in a modern Japanese school; while in the tenth chapter we shall trace the rapid transition of Japan from the darkness of mediæval feudalism to the enlightenment of the Western world. For the present we need just a clear notion of the educational methods which have made the Japan of To-Day.

The history of the Japanese people falls into three great divisions: First, the infancy of the race, extending from prehistoric times

JAPAN TO-DAY

into the third century of the Christian era; secondly, the period of Chinese culture, beginning with the alleged introduction of letters in the year 284, and continuing for fifteen centuries; and, finally, the period of European culture, which began, as has been already noted, so recently as 1854. Until this modern epoch introduced the Japan of To-Day, the educational influences had been directed wholly by Buddhism. "All education," as Professor Chamberlain has said, "was for centuries in Buddhist hands. Buddhism introduced art, introduced medicine, moulded the folk-lore of the country, created its dramatic poetry, deeply influenced politics and every sphere of social and intellectual activity. In a word, Buddhism was the teacher under whose instruction the Japanese nation grew up."

Now, as everybody knows, Buddhism is a singularly impassive and impersonal religion. One has only to study the face of the Great Buddha, as presented in an illustration in this volume, to understand the essence of Buddhistic teaching, which means self-repression, self-effacement, personal nihilism. Lanier sings, in his poem of "The Crystal,"—

The Great Buddha at Kamakura

THE CYNOSURE

" So, Buddha, beautiful! I pardon thee
That all the All thou hadst for needy man
Was Nothing, and thy Best of being was
But not to be."

Doubtless the greatest conquest, when all the odds are considered, that the great religion of India has ever made was its intellectual conquest of the Japanese. For a race less responsive by nature to such a doctrine can scarcely be imagined. They are intensely active, alert, individual; but, in obedience to the commands of the Great Nihilist, they covered their impetuous, fiery natures with the crust of a repression that ill-befitted them, thorough-going Tatars as they are.

All the more intense for this age-long repression was the activity that immediately ensued when the crust was broken, finally, in 1854. The Japanese is a born Yankee; monastic life does not become him. He had needed, however, precisely that strong self-control that came from the schooling of Buddhism. He now realized with the flash of instinct that he had finally come into his own. The ozone of the West filled his lungs. He breathed full and deep, then leaped with great bounds straight into the thick of things. The first thing that he did was to resolve to

JAPAN TO-DAY

educate himself in the ways of this new life to which he was so instantaneously responsive. In the tenth chapter we shall see in a general way how this was done. They sent an embassy around the world, to get the best that every nation had to give! In that same year the Emperor gave forth the startlingly ambitious declaration: "It is intended that henceforth education shall be so diffused that there may not be a village with an ignorant family, or a family with an ignorant member." And his intention has been amazingly fulfilled. A distinguished British journalist wrote, a few years ago, "It is so rare a thing to find, even in the lowest class, a man or woman who cannot read and write that I have no doubt the proportion of illiteracy is higher in Birmingham or in Boston than it is in Tōkyō." The figures are almost incredible, but in less than twenty years the number of pupils enrolled in the Japanese schools increased more than three million per cent. There are now enrolled in the various schools of Japan more than four and a quarter million of pupils out of a total population of some forty million. The government expends for this work annually not less than forty million

THE CYNOSURE

yen (twenty million dollars), and the various mission agencies add their thousands. Japan undertook an immense task when the Emperor issued his notable declaration in 1872. "That Japan has not miserably failed, but has succeeded in producing in thirty years a result which Russia, for example, still waits to attempt, marks her as worthy of a great future,"—so writes Mr. Lewis in his recent work, "The Educational Conquest of the Far East."

Mr. Lewis quotes an eminent Japanese educator as saying that when Japan reached out for Western ideas she copied her navy from Great Britain, her army from France, her medical science from Germany, and her educational system from America. But Mr. Henry Norman declares that the educational system of Japan is a characteristic attempt to combine in one system the Board Schools of England, the High Schools of America, the Normal Schools of France, and the Universities of Germany. Both are right. Japan chose America for her general plan, but went to other countries for specifications. The result is an elaborate system embracing five departments: (1) The Kindergartens, for very young children; (2) Elementary

JAPAN TO-DAY

Schools, which in turn are in several separate grades; (3) Middle Schools, of two classes, the Ordinary and the Higher; (4) Special Schools, the name being self-explanatory; and (5) the great University at Tōkyō, with two thousand five hundred students, the highest standards of scholarship, and famous teachers from every quarter of the globe.

"College faculties know the country boy who enters with insufficient preparation, but has accomplished such results as he could by sheer power of will and force of mind. The progress of such a boy when he finally comes under competent instructors is exhilarating. He advances by leaps, until almost before his class realizes it he is an acknowledged leader. In the great college of the nations, Japan is that boy." So writes the editor of the *Youth's Companion*. But Japan has done more than that. This rustic, unlettered boy, the minute he caught a glimpse of the world, made a flying visit to all the great schools within reach; then went back home, *built his own school,* and in a trice had caught up with the others. There is nothing like it in the history of the world. Little wonder that Japan is conceited!

THE CYNOSURE

Japanese progress in military affairs has equalled these civic advances. Mr. Norman classes the military advancement of Japan "among the modern wonders of the world. The arsenal of Koishikawa is Woolwich on a smaller scale, with a hundred rifles and seventy thousand cartridges for its day's work; the dockyard at Yokosuka is not behind Woolwich and Portsmouth in much except size, and first-rate torpedo boats and the most elaborate modern ordnance are turned out there with the regularity of Armstrong or Krupp; the Armstrong cruisers lying off Tōkyō Bay are among the finest vessels of their class afloat, and could make matchwood of many vessels here, and they are manned and officered entirely by Japanese seamen; while the War Department has at least forty thousand men under arms at this moment, and on a declaration of war could put one hundred thousand troops of all arms, and perhaps many more, in the field, with weapons equal to any carried today, all of whom would have served at least a year with the colors, and the majority for three years, and who would make a desperate fight against any army in the world. Yet twenty-five or thirty years ago Japanese

JAPAN TO-DAY

soldiers wore huge, grotesque iron-mask helmets to frighten the enemy, chain and lacquer armor to turn his blows, their great shoulder-cannon would have been antiquated in England at the time of the Armada, and they were led by a man with a fan!"

Mr. Norman wrote those words about ten years ago. No greater proof of the marvellous progress that is being made by the Japan of To-Day could possibly be given than by a contrast of Mr. Norman's figures with those which obtained on the first day of January, 1904, as furnished by the London *Times*. Permanent Army, 273,268. Reserve, 35,000. Territorial Army, 200,000. Grand total, 508,268. The same authoritative journal reports that on January 21, 1904, the Russians could not muster as against this large and well-drilled army more than 150,000 men and 266 guns, and will not be able to muster more than 200,000 men at the most. Yet Russia has been making plans for martial conquests ever since the will of Peter the Great was made cogent in 1725, while Japan is the baby among the nations.

It will be interesting also to compare the naval strength of the two combatants, side

THE CYNOSURE

by side. For these figures we are indebted to the London *Times*. (See pages 24 and 25.)

The following pages will endeavor to present the multifold aspects of the Japanese life of to-day. I have aimed to make a kaleidoscope. Japan is notoriously complex, and I leave the reader to unify the subject, if he can, from the diverse materials which I have presented as faithfully as I knew how. If my book presents a diversified appearance, then I can only say, so does Japan, and the book is by that measure true. Japan is the key to the Orient, but no one has ever found the key to Japan. What I offer is a sketch-book of views of that country which is to-day the cynosure of nations. "Sunrise-Land" will give a rapid survey of the country and the people as a whole, unified by the name of the country. "Views Awheel" and "Glimpses of Home Life" will take us from the bird's-eye view to glimpses that are caught at closer range. We shall take just a sidewise glance at the awful language, then listen to the humorous sermons of the priests. From the routine of school life in an old Southern town we shall

JAPAN TO-DAY

THE JAPANESE NAVY

Battleships	Displacement	Indicated Horsepower	Nominal Speed	Gun Protection	Weight of Broadside Fire
	Tons		Knots	Inches*	Lbs.
Hatsuse ⎫ Asahi ⎬ Shikishima ⎭	15,000	15,000	18˙0	12 (4), 6 (4)	4,240
Mikasa	15,200	16,000	18˙0	12 (4), 6 (14)	4,225
Yashima ⎫ Fuji ⎭	12,300	13,000	18˙0	12 (4), 6 (10)	4,000

Armored Cruisers	Displacement	Indicated Horsepower	Nominal Speed	Gun Protection	Weight of Broadside Fire
	Tons		Knots	Inches*	Lbs.
Tokiwa ⎫ Asama ⎭	9,750	18,000	21˙5	8 (4), 6 (14)	3,568
Yakumo	9,850	16,000	20˙0	8 (4), 6 (12), 3 (12)	3,368
Azuma	9,436	17,000	21˙0	8 (4), 6 (12), 3 (12)	3,368
Idzumo ⎫ Iwate ⎭	9,800	15,000	24˙7	8 (4), 6 (14)	3,568
Nisshin	7,700	13,500	20˙0	10 (1), 8 (2), 6 (14)	......
Kasuga	7,700	13,500	20˙0	8 (4), 6 (14)	......

Protected Cruisers	Displacement	Indicated Horsepower	Nominal Speed	Gun Protection	Weight of Broadside Fire
	Tons		Knots	Inches*	Lbs.
Takasago	4,300	15,500	˙0	8 (2), 4.7 (10), 3 (12)	800
Kasagi ⎫ Chitose ⎭	4,784	15,500	22˙5	8 (2), 4.7 (10), 3 (12)	800
Itsukushima ⎫ Hashidate ⎭	4,277	5,400	16˙7	12.5 (1), 4.7 (11)	1,260
Matsushima	4,277	5,400	16˙7	12.5 (1), 4.7 (12)	....
Yoshino	4,180	15,750	23˙0	6 (4), 4.7 (8)	780
Naniwa ⎫ Takachiho ⎭	3,727	7,120	17˙8	10.2 (2), 6 (6)	1,196
Akitsushima	3,150	8,400	19˙0	6 (4), 4.7 (6)	780
Niitaka ⎫ Tsushima ⎭	3,420	9,500	20˙0	6 (6), 3 (8)	920
Suma ⎫ Akashi ⎭	2,700	8,500	20˙0	6 (2), 4.7 (6)	355

* Number of pieces of each bore is given in parenthesis.

NOTE.—The Japanese navy includes also torpedo gunboats, 20 torpedo-boat destroyers, and 47 modern torpedo boats.

THE CYNOSURE

THE RUSSIAN NAVY

Battleships	Displacement	Indicated Horsepower	Nominal Speed	Gun Protection	Weight of Broadside Fire
	Tons		Knots	Inches*	Lbs.
Poltava } Petropavlovsk.. } Sevastopol }	10,950	11,200	17.0	12 (4), 6 (12)	3,367
Peresviet } Pobieda } Osliabia }	12,674	14,500	19.0 {	10 (4), 6 (12), 3 (20)	} 2,672
Retvisan	12,700	16,000	18.0 {	12 (4), 6 (12), 3 (20)	} 3,434
Cesarevitch	13,100	16,300	18.0 {	12 (4), 6 (12), 3 (20)	} 3,516

Armored Cruisers	Displacement	Indicated Horsepower	Nominal Speed	Gun Protection	Weight of Broadside Fire
	Tons		Knots	Inches*	Lbs.
Gromoboi	12,336	18,000	20.0	....	1,197
Bayan	7,800	17,000	22.0	....	952
Rossia	12,200	18,000	20.0	....	1,348
Rurik	10,940	13,500	18.0	....	1,345
Dmitri Donskoi	5,893	7,000	15.0	....	444

Protected Cruisers	Displacement	Indicated Horsepower	Nominal Speed	Gun Protection	Weight of Broadside Fire
	Tons		Knots	Inches*	Lbs.
Bogatyr	6,750	19,500	23.0	....	872
Askold	6,500	19,500	23.0	....	772
Varyag	6,500	20,000	23.0	....	510
Diana } Pallada } Aurora }	6,630	11,600	20.0	....	632
Boyarin	3,200	11,500	22.0	....	180
Novik	3,000	18,000	25.0	....	180

* Number of pieces of each bore is given in parenthesis.

NOTE.—The Russian navy includes also upwards of 26 torpedo-boat destroyers and 53 effective torpedo boats, many of which are effective for service in Asiatic waters. In the Black Sea are 5 battleships of the fourth class, 2 of the third class, 1 of the second class, and 1 of the first class, besides a portion of the torpedo flotilla. The fleet cannot pass the Dardanelles except in defiance of the interested Powers of Europe.

JAPAN TO-DAY

hurry to the interesting Ainu in the North. Then follow the three serious chapters with which the book shall close. We shall study Japanese traits as compared with their Chinese neighbors; we shall see by her past experience of what Japan may be capable in future; and, finally, discuss the larger meaning of the Russo-Japanese war. The Japan of the past is dead and buried. All hail to the Japan of To-Day!

II
SUNRISE-LAND

¶ The Name of Japan—Sunrise means Beauty : The Beauty of Kamakura, Enōshima, Nikkō—Sunrise means Mystery : Earthquakes, Tidal Waves, and Volcanoes—Sunrise means Light : Civilization and Christianity ; or, Manners versus Morals

II

SUNRISE-LAND

"WHAT's in a name?" It is a great mistake to think that names are meaningless, this high intimation to the contrary notwithstanding. For example, take "Japan." The word comes to us through the Dutch and the Portuguese, two peoples who had dealings with that country in very early times. Possibly the word was first introduced into Europe by a remarkable Venetian traveller named Marco Polo, who resided in China just two hundred years before that other great Italian voyager, Columbus, came to America. Polo heard the Chinese talking of a little country to the east of them, "where gold might be picked up from the streets like pebbles." They called this land Dschi-pon, and the translation from Dschi-pon to Japan is easy.

While the natives of Japan use the same alphabet as the Chinese, they give to its thousands of letters a different pronunciation. Instead of calling their country Dschi-pon,

JAPAN TO-DAY

they say "Nihon." So, by a roundabout road, "Nihon" and "Japan" come from the same starting-point. Japan is but a corruption of the native name, Nihon.

Not everybody knows this. One day a student in the government school where the writer was teaching said to me:

"Teacher, please do not call our country Japan. Call it Nihon. That is its name."

"Why?" said I; "what is the difference between calling it Nihon and calling it Japan?"

"Oh," said he, "there is a great deal of difference. The word Japan is an insult. In your country you have a black varnish which you use for veneering tin and iron. Your name for that varnish is Japan. And the reason why you foreigners call our land Japan is because you think we have just a mere varnish of civilization."

Of course I laughed over that, and told the class that there *is* a kind of varnish that we call "Japan," but we give it that name because it originated in Japan. And when I explained that Japan is, by a roundabout road, just the same as Nihon, the boys were mollified, and laughed at the patriotic ignoramus until he was red in the face.

Land of the Sunrise Beauty

SUNRISE-LAND

But—"what's in a name?" This word Japan, or Nihon, has a meaning. Note that it is of two syllables. The first is the Japanese and Chinese word for "sun;" the second syllable is their word for "source." The word Japan, then, means sun-source, sun-birth, sunrise. Japan is Sunrise-Land.

In what senses may Japan be called the Land of the Rising Sun? Leaving aside the obvious geographical fact that Japan is appropriately called Sunrise-Land because it lies so very far east, let us consider what thought is first suggested to our minds by the fact of the sunrise. Is it not a thought of beauty? Is there anything on earth more beautiful than this every-day event of the sunrise? Stand at dawn "tiptoe upon a little hill." Watch the sky clothe herself in crimson for the coming of her king. Then see him come in majesty, "rejoicing in the east," —that splendid sovereign "of this great world both eye and soul,"—and the mind is fairly thrilled with a sense of all the beauty wherewith "God the Beautiful" has blessed His splendid world. So Japan, the land of the sunrise, is a land of the sunrise beauty.

JAPAN TO-DAY

The first journey I took, on the day after landing, was by rail from Yokohama to Kamakura. We got into a little railway-car quite different from those we have at home, for it was built on the European model; the porter locked us in; a little engine gave a mighty shriek, and then glided out, through green rice-fields and across narrow streams, into the country. The miniature train hurried with a fair degree of speed through villages most picturesque, their houses thatched with straw; across rice-fields, laid out with perfect orderliness, the peasants wading knee-deep in the water; through groves of giant trees, under the bluest of blue skies, in sight of the purple mountains, onward to the ancient capital of Kamakura. Once a city of a million souls was here; now nothing but a fishing village remains, with one sole remnant of the ancient glory.

I mean the mighty Buddha. It is an image of solid bronze reared in honor of the great Gautama, who has more followers to-day than any other man that ever lived; an image which for centuries has been the Mecca of pious pilgrims from throughout the Empire. The approach is through an avenue of tall and stately trees, which give hospitable en-

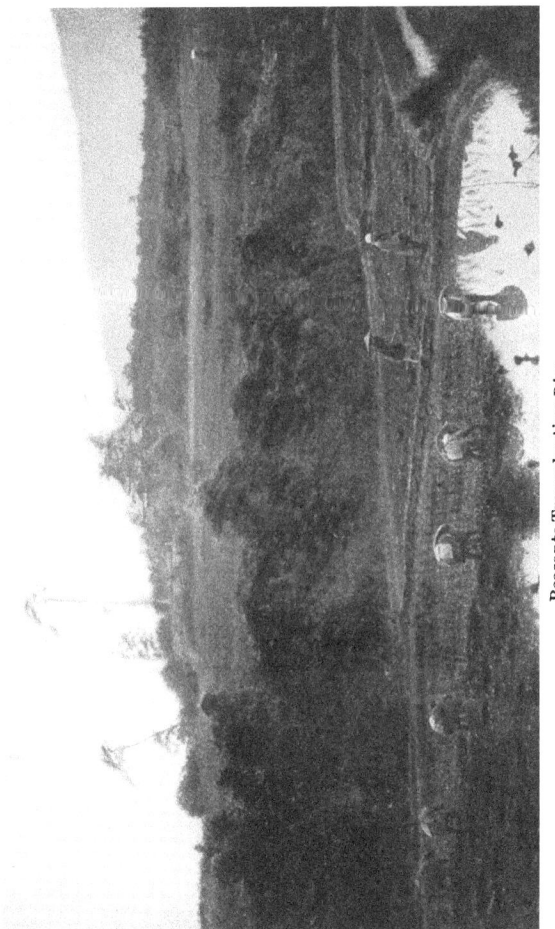

Peasants Transplanting Rice

SUNRISE-LAND

tertainment to numberless jet-black crows, cawing boldly in the branches just above us, as though well aware that all life is safe within the sacred groves of Buddha. At the end of the avenue is the idol, the most celebrated and beautiful in all this idolatrous island. Gautama is represented as sitting in a lotus flower, his hands folded placidly before him. The eyes, which are of pure gold, are cast down in modest contemplation; the entire expression is profoundly sweet and thoughtful. To get a proper idea of the size of this colossal image, you must know that it is almost fifty feet in height, or as tall as an ordinary three-story dwelling. The great, gentle mouth is over a yard in width and the ears are six feet in length. There are upon the head eight hundred and thirty curls of bronze, each nine inches long. The thumb measures three feet around, and the distance from one great folded knee to the other is nearly twelve yards. As a work of colossal art, Dai Butsu is grandly beautiful. Idol though it be, one cannot but feel a sense of awe as he looks with upturned face into the vast placid countenance of this noble Buddha, who has seen the strifes of centuries, and before whose "eternal calm" mil-

JAPAN TO-DAY

lions have bent in humble adoration. Not without meaning are the sonorous words at the gateway:

"O stranger, whosoever thou art, and whatsoever be thy creed, when thou enterest this sanctuary remember that thou treadest upon ground hallowed by the worship of ages. This is the temple of Buddha and the gate of the Eternal, and should therefore be entered with reverence."

With a feeling indeed of reverence, not for the idol itself, but for the blind yet devoted faith of millions, we turned thoughtfully away.

Out to the open sea!

In a little boat we sailed through shimmering waters to the fairy island of Enōshima, fabled to have risen from the sea in a single night. The legend is possibly true, for much of Japan is of volcanic and cataclysmic origin. The place is sacred to the goddess of Good Luck. Up the single zigzag street we climb, beset on every side by venders of beautiful shells and various other wonders of the deep. Through densely wooded summit we press to the open, with its marvellous view of the sea and the curving mainland beyond. The blue Pacific breaks white on

Fuji, the Mountain King

SUNRISE-LAND

the beach beneath us. In the distance are many white and graceful ships, skimming the waves like birds. Around us are myriad evergreens and brilliant flowers. And far, far away, swimming amid bright clouds, all his roughness lost in that enchantment lent by distance to the view, and wearing his eternal crown of snow, looms Fuji the Peerless, king of all the mountains in this mountainous land, and most perfect in form of all the mountains in the world. A perfect cone, truncated; the base lost in clouds, seemingly suspended, like some vast splendid vision, in the turquoise sky! It is a sight one can never forget.

Yet there are still more beautiful sights in this wonderful Sunrise-Land, this country where beauty abounds. The people themselves say,—

"Do not say 'Kekkō' until you have seen Nikkō!"

Kekkō means beautiful, and Nikkō is their favorite beauty spot. There is probably no other place in the whole world that combines in such marvellous degree the beauties of art with the beauties of nature. As for the landscape, it varies in impressiveness from the awful sublimity of great volcanoes to the

JAPAN TO-DAY

placid gleam of crystal lake and the boisterous rush of waterfall. One day we climbed a cliff, whence one peers timorously into an ulcered chasm wherefrom in former days the lava spouted, but where to-day seven soothing streams glide down the scarred and frowning walls, as if in gentle endeavor to smooth out the wounds of ancient battle. The town of Nikkō, founded in the year 820, finds a home for itself in the very heart of these awful hills; but the erosive power of water does its work even on the greatest heights, whence more than twenty brooks leap into bright cascades, miniature Niagaras. The largest has a fall of three hundred and fifty feet for its slender silver stream. In plain view towers the peak of Nan-Tai-Zan, more than eight thousand feet in height; its rival, Nyō-Hō-Zan, is to be seen upon the right; while in the rear stands restless Shirane, the tallest and most fearful of all the Nikkō volcanoes, which was in eruption so recently as 1889. Everywhere grow tall and stately cryptomeria, at times set out in ancient avenues many miles in length, and rivalled in our own country solely by the great trees of California.

But I spoke of the beauties of art. It is

SUNRISE-LAND

characteristic of the Japanese to seek the most beautiful surroundings for their shrines. They are notably a race of beauty-worshippers. You can visit no great mountain-peak, no large cascade, no peaceful lake, without finding there some shrine or temple to the gods of nature. It is only to be expected, then, that Nikkō should be rich in art, to match its natural wealth. Iyeyasu, the greatest Japanese of all history, finds his last resting-place where the best of nature can do him tribute with a tomb. He was buried here in 1616, and his illustrious successor, Iemitsu, keeps him solemn company. About these famous tombs great temples have been reared, which excel in prodigal magnificence anything else in Japan. A single waiting-room will sometimes represent a fortune. The most exquisite decorations in wood and silk and gold everywhere abound. In neighboring groves rise graceful pagodas, with towering monuments of stone or bronze. It is all a vast palace and a paradise. Japan the Beautiful!—Land of the Rising Sun; land of the sunrise beauty.

But the rising sun suggests to the thoughtful mind not merely the idea of beauty. As one watches the ascent of that mighty blazing ball, he is impressed also with a sense of the mystery and awesomeness of nature. What would happen should the sun for a single instant delay his ordered coming? Who upholds his vast weight? What power propels him from his bath in the eastward sea? What pilot guides him in his daily course across the sky? The sunrise, to a thoughtful mind, is suggestive of the mystery and power of nature, so that we cry with Ossian:

"Whence are thy beams, O sun—thine everlasting light? Thou comest forth in thine awful beauty,—the stars hide themselves in the sky,—the moon, cold and pale, sinks in the western wave,—thou thyself ridest alone!"

So Japan is the Land of the Rising Sun. True to its name, no land is fuller than this one of the manifestations of nature in all mystery and awful power. It is the land of the earthquake, the typhoon, the volcano, and the tidal wave. Just before our first visit the solid earth was shaken to its core, with the result that twenty-five thousand people lost their lives. Five years later, in addition to the intervening calamities, occurred a tidal wave. The waves of the sea rose in sudden anger, lashed themselves to fury, and like a

SUNRISE-LAND

roaring lion rushed with monstrous devastation across miles on miles of low-lying prostrate land, swallowing into the hungry maw of the sea no less than forty thousand human lives. A few days later, sailing along this same dread coast, we saw the dead bodies floating uncared for, there being none indeed to bury the piteous dead, save such as came from a distance for relief.

A climb up the largest active volcano in the country, and one of the largest in the world, remains fresh in memory. Seen from afar, borrowed enchantment rests upon the crest of great Asama Yama, seeming smooth and soft, while rising tall above the surrounding "mountain children," as the people love to call their hills. But draw near the lordly thing, and what seemed a pile of poetry becomes a rough, repellant mass of belched-out rock. More than eight thousand two hundred feet above the sea towers this sublime parabolic chimney, from whose throat the smoke pours out unceasingly. A hard, stiff, aching climb across the scoriated sides, through a worn-out crater whose walls are now bedecked with green, and you may look down into the great hot hole a thousand feet to where the roaring flames are seething in possession of a

JAPAN TO-DAY

secret man cannot discover. It seems a fragment of fiery hell itself. Whence this majestic, terrifying power? Nobody knows. Japan, land of the sunrise, is also the land of mystery, a country of awe and terror.

If now we pass on to speak of the people, it is still the land of the sunrise. During the past fifty years the sunlight of Western civilization has been shedding its bright light there. Not that the people had no light before—they had the moon. The civilization of the Orient, as contrasted with our own, is as moonlight compared with the sunshine. Moonlight is a very real light, and it has its advantages. It is gentle, unobtrusive, favorable to thought, to sentiment, to romance. One can but wish that the Japanese may not lose some of the gifts that have been theirs from the older days. Certainly they have nothing to learn from us in the way of etiquette. Their mutual deference is charming, and their hospitality most gracious. What could be more perfectly polite, or more expressive of the most delicate refinement, than the word for good-bye?—"*Sayonara*,"—"*If it must be so.*"

But they are feverish for the garish light of the West. Our civilization has made

SUNRISE-LAND

wonderful strides among the Japanese since Commodore Perry forced it on them at the muzzle of his sunrise guns. The Japan of To-Day is fully supplied with electric lights and telegraphs; with telephones, street-railways, and water-works. Electrical appliances are used rather more in Japan than with us. A young Japanese, looking with his American teacher at photographs of an American city, was surprised to see telegraph wires in the streets.

"Why, teacher," said he, "have those improvements actually reached America?"

He had thought they were native to Japan!

The railway service is excellent; in fact, all modes of travel are remarkably safe and swift and cheap, while there is absolutely no danger from robbery or crime. The postal department is better than our own, with free delivery at one's door even in remotest country districts, and with parcel-posts and government telegraphs at little cost. The educational system, as has been already shown, can scarcely be improved. Instead of a hundred mediocre "universities" they have just one, but that one is worthy of the name. From it as from the hub radiate colleges

JAPAN TO-DAY

and academies, lower schools and primaries, increasing in number as the grade is lowered, and all auxiliary to the single splendid centre. Newspapers are in every town, often with telegraphic service from all parts of the world. Rice exchanges and stock gambling may be found—in short, all of the latest improvements in Western civilization, including great guns and superb soldiers for killing folk. The sun of civilization has risen there. It is Sunrise-Land.

And yet, after all, Japan belies its name. Like the sunrise in its beauty, in the mystery and grandeur of its physical characteristics, and in what we call enlightenment, yes; but in the most important of all respects the people are groping and blind. And this is a most portentous anomaly. For consider, what comes to the nation that holds the priceless but perilous treasure of civilization without that wisdom to use it aright which proceeds only from moral sunshine? What came to France? The Japanese have changed in outward appearances so thoroughly that many have been deceived into believing the change complete, and that a nation can be really born

SUNRISE-LAND

in a day. The change has been phenomenal, but perhaps it has been chiefly phenomenal, and not essential. Certainly there has been no inner transformation entirely commensurate with the outward. Japan has had a Renaissance, but not a Reformation. "Over the hot and still active fires of traditional sentiment, ethnic emotions, and hereditary customs a thin crust of modern Western civilization has been laid. The crust is the appearance; the unassuaged but concealed interior fires are the dominant reality." Deceived travellers, sometimes with the best of intentions, confuse manners with morals, refinement with religion, and civilization with Christian conduct. Because they see outward polish, they argue to a change of heart, and call every cultured man a convert. They think that steamboats and railway-cars are the fruits of repentance and of godly living; and because for a season Japan had a fad for our religion, just as she has had successive fads for white rabbits and rose-bushes and sheep, we have been told that Japan is Christian and has no further need of missions. There could be no greater mistake. Travellers who spend a few weeks in the open ports go into ecstacies, but missionaries who

JAPAN TO-DAY

dwell long in the interior are tempted to fall into despair. The Japanese have beautiful manners, they have refinement, they are civilized; but they are immoral, they are not religious, they are far from being evangelized. Actual figures show that only one out of a thousand of the people can even nominally be called Christian; while the measurably true disciples do not outnumber half that sum. Is one in two thousand enough?

But I will not talk figures, and I shall not argue for the benefits of Christian missions. I will, however, cite certain instances to show the moral standing of the masses, and to explain what heathenism really means. Let us for the present pass by the fact that commercial integrity is almost unknown among the majority of Japanese merchants; that it is a rare thing for native dealers to keep their contracts; and go on to the deeper things of heart and life.

Teaching for years as I did in a government school of five hundred pupils, there were naturally rare opportunities for studying the inner life of the people, since schoolboys are often off their guard, and their teacher learns to know them as they are. As

SUNRISE-LAND

a matter of great interest to me, I once gave the classes in English composition this subject for their essays,—" The Noblest Thing I Ever Heard of." I wished to discover the ideals of Japanese boys. What things do they deem noble and good and true? Who are their heroes? What are their best views of life?

The China-Japan war had just closed. It will be remembered that one of the last incidents of that war was the seizure by the Japanese navy of the Chinese fleet, which had been under the command of Admiral Ting. Now, the better classes of Chinese and Japanese have the same ultimate basis of heathen "morality,"—namely, Confucianism. Confucianism may be said to have only one article in its creed,—filialism,—which it extends and applies to the State. It teaches that a man's highest duty is to his ruler—above wife, above children, above father and mother, above right, and even above the Almighty. Therefore, when Admiral Ting's fleet was surrounded, he surrendered it promptly enough; but he felt that it would be a supreme disgrace to His Majesty the Emperor of China to have one of his highest officials, Ting himself, fall into the hands of the

JAPAN TO-DAY

enemy. Ting therefore killed himself, out of respect for his Emperor.

What would have been the feelings of the North for Robert E. Lee if, at Appomattox, rather than share the fate of the gallant men he had surrendered, he had committed suicide from a sense of devoted patriotism? Instead of admiring him for the unsullied hero and knightly character that he was, North and South alike would have despised him. And yet nine out of ten of my Japanese schoolboys wrote of the suicide of Admiral Ting as the noblest thing of which they had ever heard. If a suicide is their ideal, and if *hara-kiri* is the best thing they know of, what shall we suppose is the worst? This sentiment of laudation for Ting was voiced in every paper in the country, and by every public teacher, by priests and by people alike, so far as I could learn. The highest morality they possess encourages self-destruction.

This system of ethics teaches that, next to the State, one owes his duty to his parents. That has a pleasant enough sound; Japanese filial piety is a very attractive phrase indeed. But here is an illustration of what it sometimes means in practice. Just after we landed, the newspapers were full of the

SUNRISE-LAND

story of an ignorant peasant in the interior, who was greatly troubled in mind by the fact that his aged mother seemed to be losing her sight. He tried many remedies, all in vain. Then he sought the assistance of his religion. He went to a priest, perchance to a so-called wizard, and asked for advice on the subject. Filialism being vital, the oracle inquired:

"Are you willing to do anything to save your mother's sight that the gods may require?"

"Yes," the poor man said, "I am."

Then the hideous answer came,—

"Feed her a human liver, and her sight will be restored."

A very shrewd answer, one would say, because it could not be obeyed; and in justice to the oracle, it may be said that there was probably no expectation that the man's filial piety would stand such a test as that. But the devout peasant was in deadly earnest. It never occurred to him to question the divine origin or wisdom of this message; he had implicit faith. And his devoutness prompted him to execute it.

The only possibility of testing the fiendish remedy was by slaying one of his own household. He had but one child, a mere babe.

JAPAN TO-DAY

His love for his child was great; for whatever else may be said of the Japanese, they are certainly not "without natural affection," like the Romans in the time of St. Paul. This man, however, was more than a father; he was a religious devotee. His religious feeling of devotion to his mother, and his fear of the avenging gods, determined his conduct along the line of the only "morality" he knew. One night he took his sleeping child out into the little garden, and was about to slay it with a knife. But in some way the wife and mother heard, and understood. She begged the man to spare the child. He told her the words of the oracle; he reminded her of the supreme demands of filial piety, and while she agreed with him in the theory of it all, her mother-love was stronger with her than anything else in the world, and she implored him to spare her child. But the man was inexorable.

"Oh," said she, at last, "if the gods must be obeyed, take me; but save my baby."

At length he yielded to this request. The child's life was spared. But the wife died at her husband's hands, and the gods were satisfied.

Mother and Child

SUNRISE-LAND

Is it not a fearful thing to see one of the holiest feelings of humanity, this sentiment of filial piety, made into a horror at which devils well might shudder? But the strangest part of my story is yet to come. I said that nine out of ten of these pupils wrote of the suicide of Admiral Ting as the noblest deed of which they had ever heard. One of them, however, actually chose the deed that has just been described,—not the self-sacrifice of the mother, but the inhuman sacrifice on the part of the husband and father. Doubtless the deed had been held up to the lad by his ignorant parents at home, or perchance by his parish priest, as an example in filial piety worthy to be ranked among the exploits of the "Four and Twenty Paragons."* The murder of his wife by that benighted man, out of devotion to the aged mother—this because filialism was the only morality he knew—was the noblest deed my lad had ever heard of.

I have not dwelt upon the vices of the Japanese. I have not spoken of their lying, because that is a vice from which we "shrewd" Americans are by no means free. I have not

* A classic collection of filial stories for the moral edification of youth.

JAPAN TO-DAY

spoken of their licentiousness, because even our public prints too often prove that there are unclean in the camp here with us. But let us thank God that at least we have worthy ideals, even though we fall in the dust far below them. And may He have pity on those "enlightened" folk across the sea, whose very ideals may be badges and tokens of shame! Suicide and wife-murder,—if this be their "morality," what is their immorality? Are they in the sunshine, or the darkness? Japan is indeed a beautiful land, the home of a charming people. But Japan is also a land of gloom, where the people are sitting in darkness amid the terrible shadows of sin.

Yet I would not finish this "sunrise" sketch in such dark colors. The sun of righteousness is not yet risen on Japan, but the streaks of dawn are glimmering there. Among those multitudes who "love the darkness," the "children of light" are already sparsely intermingled; few, but mighty in their influence. The gospel has shown itself a divine power for the salvation of men in the Orient as well as here in the West. I have seen men turned from darkness to light by the simple

SUNRISE-LAND

story of Christ's cradle and cross, lisped by the lips of children. There was Mizoguchi; a man whose life was so evil that it marked him for wickedness even among his heathen neighbors. His children began coming to a little street Sunday-school, where they learned to sing our sweet Christian songs,— the words being translated, of course, but the tunes the same that are sung the wide world over. At home he heard this singing, and he liked the music, but the words were strange. They were mysterious words to him; words of "the sweet old story," of the "heart that is whiter than snow," of a God who loves and a Christ that saves. So, finally, one morning he came with his children, curious to hear the meaning of these songs. He heard; he believed; and now for more than seven years he has been a faithful member of the church in Saga. "A little child shall lead them." There, as here, the gospel is "the power of God unto salvation to every one that believeth."

Nowhere does it show its power more than on the death-bed. I have seen it triumph over the "king of terrors" more than once, in a land where death means *death,* where only the few scattered Christians have the hope of

JAPAN TO-DAY

a life beyond death. There was Soejima, a man fifty years old, who, through the work of our own infant mission, at last found faith in God. A year afterwards he was taken ill. One bright Sunday our little company of Christians were gathered about the communion table, in a chapel near his house. He had been left at home in bed. We were mightily surprised, while in the act of communing, to see him, gaunt and tottering, approaching up the aisle, supporting himself by the ends of the rude benches on either side. He fell on his knees at the altar and received the sacrament. Friends bore him home in their arms. A few days later we were called to see him in his final hour. Sadly worn and thin was his poor racked frame, but it was thrilled with a delight that death could not take from him. Wan was his dying face, yet bright with a smile that really set death at naught. Hollow his eyes and dim, yet the last light in them was the most beautiful, for it had the touch of heaven's own radiance. He died trustful and glad.

I recall also young Hamasaki, struck down in the strength and pride of his youth with a loathsome and hopeless malady. He also had found faith in Christ and His resurrection.

SUNRISE-LAND

I hold in my hand, while writing, a little Japanese Testament that he gave me on a Christmas day just before his death. On the fly-leaf, in his struggling English, are the words: " Please accept my little Plesent. Hamasaki." As he lay dying, he found strength to say, with his very latest breath, the simple prayer, " Take me!"—lifting his hand the while, which the Great Shepherd did indeed take, to lead him through the valley of the shadow. Mother and sister and brother could not resist the parable of that death. They sought the same power for their own lives, and through his death were led to life.

But I will not go on. Instances could be multiplied to show that the first faint dawn is gleaming in that Eastern land, even amid the darkness of the masses; while in a closing chapter I shall show that Christian influences have been steadily moulding the leadership of new Japan, albeit unrecognized at times. But the full sunrise is yet to come. God speed the day!

III
VIEWS AWHEEL

¶ Tōkyō in the Rain—A Jinrikisha Ramble—The Wheel-
man's Paradise—Bishop Potter
at Nagasaki

III

Views Awheel

Had Bayard Taylor only owned a bicycle or had access to a jinrikisha, he would not have called his charming traveller's sketch-book "Views Afoot." I am obliged to him for having suggested to me a title for this chapter that has the added distinction of association with such a masterpiece as his.

Some long-suffering British resident, having exhausted his prose vocabulary during the prolonged "rainy season" of the late spring and early summer, suddenly dropped into poetry "with a dull and sickening thud," as follows:

> " Dirty days hath September,
> April, June, and November;
> From February unto May
> The rain it raineth every day;
> All the rest have thirty-one,
> Without one blessed gleam of sun,
> And if any of 'em had two-and-thirty
> They'd be just as wet and twice as dirty."

JAPAN TO-DAY

"It has been raining continuously for the past twenty-four hours, and continually since my arrival in Tōkyō a month ago,"—this was the first report I sent home concerning the Japanese climate. From my window I could watch the little Japanese women, and scarcely larger men, tottering along on their stilted wooden shoes, which lift them above the mud; under their paper umbrellas, which keep them dry. The idea of a paper umbrella may appear ridiculous to a Western mind, but that is because the average Western mind is unacquainted with the qualities of Japanese paper. Many a time have I walked through a heavy rain under the shelter of these frail roofs, without being wet in the least. The paper is stubbornly fibrous, rendered impervious to rain and strongly resistant to rents.

Within two feet of my window was a beautiful, brave little palm-tree, which has learned, in whatsoever state it is, therewith to be content. It kisses the rain, smiles to the sun, and caresses the wind forever. It wraps its delicate body up from the cold in a natural coat of hair, and thus keeps itself green all the winter. I came soon to look upon it as a bright and happy companion, teaching

VIEWS AWHEEL

a sweet, constant lesson of contentment. Through the branches of this cheery little tree I see two of my largest cherry-trees. Each year they bloom into fragrance and beauty, to become the delight of this beauty-loving people, who cherish the flower and ignore the fruit. The plum-trees, too, are covered with rich, fleecy pop-corn, and little shrubs blossom daintily everywhere of which I do not even suspect the name.

Beyond the trees are the palings, then the street, in which I catch glimpses of a jet-haired maiden with dark, liquid eyes and rosy-red cheeks, and a baby brother on her bending shoulders. She is laughing now— she is laughing almost always—and the child is merry with her. There go three other girls, laughing. It is well that they are merry now, for their joyousness may go full soon. Wifehood here is slavery, and only in old age does relief return.

Across the street is one of the little shops —of which the city is full—where you may buy stamps and register your letters. Like all the other shops, it is wooden, unpainted, one-story, and ugly It has glass sliding doors, but you do not need to go in, for near the door is a hole like a ticket-office, where

JAPAN TO-DAY

you can communicate with the authorities and transact your business.

Next to the little post-shop is a livery-stable, with men instead of horses, and jinrikishas for buggies. You can hire a single team for eight *sen* per hour, though if you are a "griffin," or what the college boys call a "rat," you will probably pay double.

My house is on a corner, and my study really has two windows instead of one. I move now to the other, and see stretching before me, just beyond a narrow, bridged canal, an exceptionally wide street, which is well macadamized. Commanding a view of this street and the rest of the neighborhood, and within speaking distance from my window, is a little box-like house with glass on every side. In front of it there stands or treads perpetually a martial man in handsome uniform, with gold-embroidered cap and shining sword. There are four of these men in this tiny station-house, relieving each other by turns. They are the guardians of the peace; but as the peace always seems to guard itself, their main service is to make an impression. The one they make on me is favorable. I like them, for they are polite and friendly.

Japanese Landscape Gardening

VIEWS AWHEEL

Off there to the left, bordering the wide street, one sees a large public garden. In one corner there is a huge mound, covered with trees and with grasses. Elsewhere an artificial stream threads its way under artificial rustic bridges, and all about us are evidences of wonderful skill in the art of landscape gardening, one of the numerous arts in which the deft Japanese excel. In this capital city of Tōkyō there are four great parks, widely celebrated, known as Shiba, Asakusa, Uyeno, and the Kudan. Shiba is the most beautiful in point of gloomy majesty, which dwells in the lofty pines; and Asakusa is fullest of true human interest. I wish the children that read this might have gone with me there some fine day to see the sights of the great gay market, where silk and sawdust elephants hobnob with stuffed herons, and painted oscillating monsters swing in little bamboo trees, and the most life-like dolls in the world make one smile at their "cute" humanity. There is, besides, a great museum and a garden of zoölogy, where the funniest monkey I ever saw makes faces at you, and a ferocious tiger growls for bloody meat. Then, there are the shows, with the open stage exposed to the street,—stages

JAPAN TO-DAY

whereon boy jugglers balance themselves in impossible postures and dance upon rolling balls. And there is the temple, grand and gilded, with horrible statues guarding the gates, and the poor mistaken people praying to their senseless idols.

What is that great building on that faraway hill, scarcely visible through the mists of the rain? Doubtless some government building, constructed, they tell us, after the most approved style of foreign architecture, which must mean, one suspects, that it is foreign to all known styles of architecture. You may see many such here in Tōkyō, for the administration is constructive in its policy. There to the right is a skyward-climbing tower, from the top of which curls a smoky column. It is the great chimney of some iron factory, and it also has its many fellows in this wondrous Oriental town.

Yes, it is raining, raining, raining, as though we were indeed to be deluged. But the sight-seer is largely independent of the weather in this most obliging country. For are there not the jinrikishas?—literal little "pull-man-cars," as the word denotes,—and will not our human horses come to the very doorstep, and tuck us snugly in, and pull the

Rain-coats made of Straw

VIEWS AWHEEL

oilcloth curtains up in front and behind, so that we remain as dry as ever we please? So come, without further ado, and go with me for true "views awheel" through the streets of this marvellous city! Peering out from within our sheltered carriages, we see peasants and coolies hurrying along in their funny rain-coats, which are nothing but great bundles of rice-straw draped from their shoulders; and the sight makes us selfishly but deliciously comfortable as we settle ourselves back on the cushions.

The way of our human horses is temporarily obstructed, even in the streets of a great city like this, through the general habit the people have of walking in the middle of the road. Only on a few thoroughfares is there any excuse for a sidewalk; and even there the pedestrians persist in their habit. The jinrikishaman, who always goes in a trot, is ceaselessly ejaculating a jerky little "*Hi!*" which serves as a warning to those in his way; a warning always heeded with good nature. The streets are in most cases narrow, short, and running in all directions. There is no order in the plan of the city. Consequently, you get lost within a few yards of home until you learn the landmarks, which themselves

JAPAN TO-DAY

are often like the traditional needle in the haystack. It is difficult for a stranger to see any difference in the hundreds of little streets, each with its many doorless shops,—like a face without eyelids,—wherein are displayed to full view the entire stock-in-trade of the thievish merchants. My use of this unpleasant word is sadly appropriate; for only in shops conducted upon foreign principles is the new-comer safe from extortion. The genuine Japanese merchant always asks double for his wares, and sometimes treble; then the purchaser is expected to conduct the demoralizing process vulgarly known as "Jewing-down." This custom has given rise to a special class of idioms, to which a chapter in every grammar is devoted. I never once entered a Japanese shop alone without sore quailings of courage and a pretty definite conviction that I should pay two prices for my purchases. However, all the native articles are sold at such an extremely low rate as somewhat to atone for the extortionate greed of the seller.

Only on the Ginza—the Broadway of this Japanese New York—are the stores at all pretentious, and even there they compare unfavorably with the structures found in our

VIEWS AWHEEL

smaller towns at home. On the Ginza I recall a street-car line—served by poor horses with two legs apparently in the grave—and frequent omnibuses. Beyond these commodities, the use of beasts of burden is but seldom seen, since men are the heavy-laden in Japan. Not to speak of the ubiquitous jinrikisha, it is a common sight to see two or four men pulling and pushing an unconscionably heavy load of farm products or of lumber up a steep hill, while the perspiration drips from their swarthy half-clothed frames, and their already tried lungs sound out a not unmusical ejaculation with every alternate step. Such extravagant waste of breath, indulged presumably for the purpose of keeping in step, if musical, is surely in a minor key; for it is difficult to conceive any sound more plaintive than this of ceaseless vocalized weariness.

The business of pulling this little carriage in which we ride has grown to great magnitude in Japan, many families being dependent for their daily bread upon the exertions of the poor, trotting, hard-worked human horse that goes so patiently and faithfully between the shafts. These laborers are, indeed, so numerous as to constitute a distinct

JAPAN TO-DAY

class; there are thirty thousand of them in Tōkyō alone, and it is impossible to walk fifty yards without having one approach you and respectfully solicit employment. They are for the most part quite indigent, yet their scanty income is diminished the more by a tax required for the governmental treasury. The law also compels them to wear a sort of uniform, and is strictly enacted with regard to certain other regulations. Their condition is certainly such as to excite our pity, which would be quite unallayed were it not that these overworked men are such incorrigible swindlers. If you fail to make your bargain in advance, there is sure to be a quarrel when the journey is at an end, because of the exorbitant rate demanded; and often, even though the bargain was duly made before the ride began, the time of final reckoning becomes unpleasant through the insatiable demands of the coolie. He is especially fond of imposing upon new-comers. A friend of mine, when first arriving in Yokohama, paid eighty *sen* for an hour's ride—just ten times the legal rate!

While we have been talking about these avaricious but indispensable workmen, they have drawn us swiftly through these narrow,

VIEWS AWHEEL

labyrinthine streets of Tōkyō, where the strange sights are quite too numerous to mention; past great government buildings, across canals, and over the Ginza to the imperial castle walls, just as the sun comes out from the mists to lighten the beautiful landscape. These walls are of massive stone, reared from ten to twenty feet in height, or else made of great embankments, upon which the grass is growing fresh and beautiful. Beneath the wall is dug a deep canal, which serves the more effectually to debar all possible invaders. These welded walls and moats enclose great spaces in the centre of the city, wherein is yet another similar defensive structure, inside which, all out of sight, is the Mikado's own sacred palace. As one cannot get a glimpse of this palace without indefinite trouble, we must content ourselves with a ride or two around the inner wall, and pass on to other sights; leaving behind us the handsome Teikoku Hotel, one of the finest hostelries in the East, fitted as it is with all the modern improvements, and charging immoderate rates.

It is surely a scene of rare beauty, as we pass once more around the walls. The shrubbery is luxuriant in rich vernal vest-

JAPAN TO-DAY

ure, the rare sunlight gleams on the placid waters of the moat, wherein hundreds of unmolested water-fowl are happy just because they are living,—while about us Plato's gaily dressed "featherless bipeds" chatter and laugh in their merry and careless fashion.

More jogging through crowded streets,—in mortal fear lest our men run over a toddling baby or two,—and we pass the entrance to the great Asakusa Park, with its handsome Buddhist temple, one of the largest and most popular in the country. There is no time to enter. With a gaze of interest at the tall red pagoda, towering so gracefully towards the sky, we pass on through the straggling suburbs into the country itself. All along the route we see tiny shrines and images of the great Dai Butsu, whose chief original, at Kamakura, was described in a former chapter.

There go two interesting characters! Their heads are shaven, and you will note they are clad most handsomely, for they are wearing their festival garments. They are none other than Buddhist priests, of whom there are thousands in this priest-ridden country. They are young, and have bright, attractive faces.

VIEWS AWHEEL

See the rice-fields! At this season they are flooded with water, which is conducted, in some cases, for a great distance. Everything in Japan is laid out on a tiny scale, except the cities and the mountains. The fields are strikingly small and toy-like, and it is easy to imagine the people whom we see at work to be children playing in the mud. Queer people in queer garments, working for their daily bread! If the rice crop fails, as it did a few years ago, woe to dependent Japan! Her strength lies mainly in this nutritive cereal, which constitutes almost the sole diet of the people. In former years it was the money of Japan: everything was bartered in rice. On the other side of the road one sees acres planted in tea, which grows in low, bunchy bushes, dark green and fragrant. Between the rows of the precious stuff, men and women are stooping to gather with care the leaves, which are cured, sorted, and shipped to our tea-pots at home. Besides the tea and rice crops of Japan, the country produces opulent harvests of barley, millet, and beans, with smaller quantities of cotton and tobacco. Agriculture is as yet conducted almost wholly by hand, labor being cheap and abundant. The methods of cultivation are primitive, but thorough. Fertilization is extensively (and offensively) employed. Vegetables such as we use are uncommon, and if seeds are imported, they produce good results, but fail to transmit reproductive power to their offspring—that is, fresh seed must be imported every year. The chief fruits are the persimmon, orange, and *biwa*, the latter being a small and strange yellow plum. Exotic fruits almost always lack the flavor to which we are accustomed here at home—such as the fig, the peach, and the apple, which are produced in very small quantity, with the possible exception of the fig. Small fruits, however, can be raised in abundance, and well flavored. The northernmost island of Yezo has offered best opportunity for experiments in advanced agriculture.

And now we *have* met an interesting group! It is a family in travel. The mother has one baby bundled on her back, while the father carries another in a basket which is suspended from a stick swung across his shoulder! He is wearing a stiff, wide, white-cloth hat, made like an overturned basin, and is smoking a tiny pipe that gives only three whiffs for one filling. A Japanese likes noth-

A Family Journey

VIEWS AWHEEL

ing better than to be continually refilling and relighting his pipe. But our "pull-man-cars" hurry us on, and we have time for but a glimpse of two or three Japanese maidens, sitting on their heels in a tea-house, eating their mid-day meal. Of course they eat with chop-sticks, which are much more easily used than one would think. Their table is a few inches high, the dishes are saucers, and the tea-cups are like so many big thimbles. They laugh aloud at the funny foreigners, but in such a sweet, soft voice that we cannot find it in us to feel offended.

Now we meet a man with a veritable conservatory on his shoulders! Yes; the flower-men of Japan dispose their beautiful wares on two platforms, which are suspended at either end of a pole. The man gets under the pole, and goes through the streets and along the road crying out his bargains to the beauty-loving people, who prize flowers more than we prize fruit. Let us buy a few bunches for half as many cents, and hurry once more homewards.

"Jitensha" is the Japanese for bicycle, and is flung a hundred times a day from

JAPAN TO-DAY

the healthy throats of the little Japs as they watch the gliding wheels. It means a man-propelling vehicle; and Japan is the wheelman's paradise.

There are roads as smooth as a race-track dissecting the pygmy rice-fields, skirting the bamboo thickets, invading the dale and the forest, gently climbing the graded hill, with a dash down the other side. There are kindly people, comfortable and unique lodgings, helpful tinkers in case of need, and a porousness of soil that takes the moisture from the earth in less time than it took the rain to fall. Upon the fact that the Japanese are a barefoot race, and do their own hauling, rests a most happy benefit to the pneumatic tire. The coolie keeps the road free from sharp stones, and thus saves many a puncture to his feet and to our tires. Surely there are few countries more inviting to the man that loves his wheel than is this Mikado's land.

And yet our paradise is not without its snares. Perhaps the chief nuisance we have to encounter is the ubiquity of babies and dogs. The dog can usually be taught his place by a skilful kick, but we have to look out for the babies. Their mothers permit them to spend the entire day in the middle of

VIEWS AWHEEL

the streets, and we do not care to macadamize the roads with them. It takes a serious exertion of lung-power to make a baby overcome his astonishment; and then, when he does begin to move, like as not he toddles squarely along in front of you. Sometimes he will be standing quietly at the side of the road when all of a sudden he makes a sickening dash directly across your path. But you cannot be vexed with him; he is far too "cute" and charming for that, with his queer little oldish clothes, his rosy, chubby cheeks, and his half-shaved head. The baby Jap, God bless him; he torments us, but we love him still!

There are other features that add a zestful tang to the delights of this delectable wheelman's-land. Sometimes one runs across a long piece of road that has lately been repaired according to Oriental methods, and the sensation is anything but heavenly. This method consists in dumping a heap of loose, round pebbles into the thoroughfare, and leaving the rest to nature. Or, again, the adventurous spirit may dare to take a mountain road, and suffer for his daring.

I well remember an occasion of this kind, when a party of us went across from Tōkyō

JAPAN TO-DAY

to Atami by the mountain passage. Atami is a village by the sea beyond the mountains, where there are hot baths and geysers. As dusk came on we had a looming mountain between us and Atami, when a howling wind came out against us and blew out our lamps, leaving us in Egypt darkness. There was no help for it, so we called at a peasant's hut and ate some sweet bean-cakes with the inevitable tea, and after that began the ascent.

Oh, the long, rough, dusty, windy climb to the top! How heavy the wheels were! A little night-bird sat amid a thicket of waving bamboo and exasperated us by screaming in our native tongue, "Git thar! git thar! git thar!" We got there at last—to the top. The wind was blowing harder. At the edge of the road, which was not an inch over six feet wide, one could stand and peer through the darkness down towards the base of this precipice, where he could hear the lash of the angered sea, hundreds of feet sheer beneath him. The descent was exceedingly steep, but we coasted in the teeth of the wind and in the face of the midnight darkness, because we were tired, and hardly cared whether we were blown over the edge or not. Several times, indeed, we were forced to dismount. But by

VIEWS AWHEEL

ten o'clock the long ride was over, and we can never forget the deliciousness of that steaming natural bath, fresh from the throat of the geyser, with the rough rub-down and the supper—especially the supper!—and the beds. Next day it was over the peaks again, but we were sensible enough to have the coolies tow our wheels with ropes flung over their shoulders, for a long, rough trip was before us. Now do not scorn us for hiring those coolies, pray, because the ascent was fearfully steep, leading over a stony, untrodden path. When at length we reached the top,—there "we saw the full glory of the Lord. Great Fuji towering, snow-capped, eight thousand feet above, and the blue Pacific flecked with sails four thousand feet below, and all the spurs of land and tiny plateaux were covered with garden farms and toy-like villages.

"But the wheelman cannot stop long. Waiting is not his virtue. The coolies are paid off, and we glance at the road. It winds down with longer curves and gentler. Then we examine brakes, and find them, too, all right. So, feet on coasters, brake well in hand, and away! For miles and miles we coast down the curving mountain-side. It is a holiday, and the peasants are resting from

JAPAN TO-DAY

their labors. They see us far above, and line their village streets, all dressed in their best; silent, respectful, hesitant, as the strange procession of visitants from the clouds glides past.

"Down we go for miles, and then one brief stretch of level ground brings us to our nooning place. Our welcome over, we are led to a suite of clean, white-matted rooms in the second story, overlooking the tiny garden full of quaint shrubs and trees. Barefooted, deft-handed maidens bring lacquer trays with dainty dishes full of soup, rice, fish, and eggs, with chopsticks, best of implements for such fare, and bountiful supply of fragrant, straw-colored tea. So we rest an hour content, at the foot of Fuji San, before the wheels go on again."

Before that journey was over we had wheeled several hundred miles, at least those of us had that finished; for out of nine starters there were only three to complete the journey. Our original party embraced Americans, Englishmen, and a Russian; business men, missionaries, and a diplomatist. The diplomat's name was Boughkovetsky, which defied us, so we compromised and called him "Bottle-o'-whiskey." This was

Typical Country Scene—a Tea Plantation

VIEWS AWHEEL

not inappropriate, seeing he was famous for good spirits. We consumed quantities of milk, for which we contracted in advance by telegraph, as the people themselves do not use it. Everywhere there was nothing but gentleness and friendliness and harmless curiosity.

It was a sight to ride through the earthquake region, where the earth broke open only a few months before and thousands perished. We crossed a bridge bent like a series of "switchbacks" by the terrific upheaving force. We saw the wretchedness of the sufferers bemoaning their dead, while their fallen homes lay before them. One dismal night, after the ferryman had lost us on the river, we came into an inn where foreigners had surely never lodged before. They brought us their wadded quilts for beds, and little wooden anvils for pillows, and raw meat to eat. We ate it and slept. What is there a hungry, tired wheelman cannot do?

There are many foreign riders in Japan, as well as natives. The machine is especially useful to the missionary, for with it he can penetrate to the remotest regions at far more rapid pace than that of the jinrikishaman,

JAPAN TO-DAY

and save the fees that must otherwise be paid. Consequently, and because pleasure may be so admirably combined with work, there are but few missionaries without a wheel.

When my home was in the southern island of Kyūshū, I frequently rode across the mountains to the port of Nagasaki, where the great white "Empresses" of the Canadian Pacific fleet pause for fresh supplies of fuel before plunging into the yellow waters of the China Sea. Here may be witnessed a remarkable scene, which has been sketched with such graphic skill by the sympathetic hand of Bishop Potter that I venture to transfer it bodily from the pages of his suggestive little book, "The East of To-Day and To-Morrow."

"If I were asked to say," declares Bishop Potter, "of all that I saw in Japan, what that is that lives most vividly in my memory, I should probably shock my artistic reader by saying that it was the loading of a steamship at Nagasaki with coal. The huge vessel, the *Empress of Japan,* was one morning, soon after its arrival at Nagasaki, suddenly festooned—I can use no other word—from stem to stern on each side with a series of hanging platforms, the broadest nearest the base and

VIEWS AWHEEL

diminishing as they rose, strung together by ropes, and ascending from the *sampans,* or huge boats in which the coal had been brought alongside the steamer, until the highest and narrowest platform was just below the particular port-hole through which it was received into the ship. There were, in each case, all along the sides of the ship, some four or five of these platforms, one above another, on each of which stood a young girl. On board the *sampans* men were busy filling a long line of baskets holding, I should think, each about two buckets of coal, and these were passed up from the *sampans* in a continuous and unbroken line until they reached their destination, each young girl, as she stood on her particular platform, passing, or rather almost throwing, these huge basketfuls of coal to the girl above her, and she again to her mate above her, and so on to the end. The rapidity, skill, and, above all, the rhythmic precision with which, for hours, this really tremendous task was performed was an achievement which might well fill an American athlete with envy and dismay. As I moved to and fro on the deck above them, watching this unique scene, I took out my watch to time these girls, and again and again

JAPAN TO-DAY

I counted sixty-nine baskets—they never fell below sixty—passed on board in this way in a single minute. Think of it for a moment. The task—I ought rather to call it an art, so neatly, simply, and gracefully was it done—was this: the young girl stooped to her companion below her, seized from her uplifted hands a huge basket of coal, and then, shooting her lithe arms upward, tossed it laughingly to the girls above her in the ever-ascending chain. And all the while there was heard, as one passed along from one to another of these chains of living elevators, a clear, rhythmical sound, which I supposed at first to have been produced by some bystander striking the metal string of something like a mandolin, but which I discovered after a little was a series of notes produced by the lips of these young coal-heavers themselves—distinct, precise, melodious, and stimulating. And at this task these girls continued, uninterruptedly and blithely, from ten o'clock in the morning until four o'clock in the afternoon, putting on board in that time, I was told, more than one thousand tons of coal. I am quite free to say that I do not believe that there is another body of workfolk in the world who could have performed

VIEWS AWHEEL

the same task in the same time and with the same ease."

It is not only an interesting sight, it is also most suggestive, as the sage Bishop has thoughtfully observed. Japan has seized the wonderful implements of our Western civilization, and she is using them in her own original manner, after methods unknown to us, impossible to us, and startling by their Oriental novelty. Her naval tactics in the present war are striking examples of this interesting fact. As was indicated in the opening chapter, her wonderful ability to receive and her marvellous agility to apply our Western implements of power give to her little people, few though they be in number, a most important position in the immediate development of history. What will happen when her ponderous Amazonian sister across the Yellow Sea shall have learned from this pygmy genius the secrets of our Saxon strength and progress? What will happen if Russia shall fail in this war, bringing about the China-Japan alliance as an established fact, as it is now the cherished dream of some of the foremost statesmen of either empire? Is the "yellow peril" a sensational phantom of the "yellow press," or

JAPAN TO-DAY

is the problem of phlegmatic China to be solved through the tutorship of the nimble Japanese? A consideration of these interesting questions will be offered in the closing chapter of this book. Questions like these troop insistently and continually through the maze of marvellous scenes that bewilder and confuse the traveller in the mystical, brooding East.

IV
GLIMPSES OF HOME LIFE

¶ In a Japanese Home—The Children—Festivals and Myths —The Women—Christian Wedlock, so-called

IV

GLIMPSES OF HOME LIFE

IT was an uncertain April morning. April days are uncertain everywhere, but in Japan they are very uncertain. As I started, gray clouds were scurrying, "quick-footed," as the idiom is, across the sky; but the all-wise cook said, "As for showering, it will not be." My bicycle was a new sight in the old Southern town. Many an *"O-rya!"* of amaze popped out as it spun through the narrow streets; many a cry of *"Bikkuri!"*—"You scared me!"—was followed by a scarcely less astonished *"Oto-denshin!"*—"Noiseless!" The discovery of silent wheels, so different from the clattering jinrikishas, surprised these loin-girt pedestrians into their most rustic dialect. None but Saga men could understand that *Oto-denshin*. Their idioms are most peculiar. The Tōkyō word for "No" is the Saga word for "Yes."

But I was forgetting the April day. Cook San was a prophet: as for showering, it was not. But wind! How it swirls on you from the hills, pressing you back as with a strong hand on the breast, and filling your eyes with sand! And the mud! Where there came a clayey stretch of road, the wheels would not go round, and there was but one thing to do —shoulder them. Then the wind passed, the roads relented, and my thirty miles (after a race with a tiny coal-train) had brought me to the sea. Karatsu is beautiful: the wedding of the mountains with the ocean makes it so. The hills run down into the blue Pacific, and a long stretch of mountain-pines lave their bold feet in the tides. On yonder truncated knob, clad now in clouds of cherry-blossoms, lies the ruin of one of the strongest of ancient castles, whence the strongest of feudal chiefs defied his foes. A few miles to the south is the important little port of Sasebo, a key to the present naval situation in Japan. And here in the road is Suzuki, with a bow in his hand, who starts and smiles as he sees me.

Suzuki is a big, open-hearted student of the Saga government school, at home for the spring vacation. I had liked him, and he liked me well enough to do what is done very rarely in Japan,—inviting me, a foreigner and a Christian, to spend several days in his

HOME LIFE

home, where alien had never yet set foot. Inns there are a-plenty; but seldom do the pagan homes open to Western guests for a visit of days. I trundled my wheel beside him, to the clatter of many clogs, which scampered away if I but turned,—chiefly little girls, their backs bent with the weight of sleeping babies.

I make myself ridiculous when in the house. When my shoes are off, and I stand on the spotless mats, there come the mother, the sister, the cousin, the brothers, to give me welcome. As they all bob down and butt their heads on the floor, what am I to do? To stand is insufferable, so I bob and butt too. But with what sad lack of grace! They do it gracefully enough,—*they* stoop and bow; a foreigner never does. It is a serious question, this of the native etiquette. "And is there not an honorable weariness?"—"He came by the self-rolling vehicle!"—"The roads of Nippon are indeed very inconvenient for you."—"And the sky-humor is to-day very changeable!" A different language from my own, and different customs, truly; but the hospitality there is no mistaking. As one of their proverbs says, "Humanity is the same the world over."

JAPAN TO-DAY

They bring my meal to me on lacquered tables a foot high and square, before which one squats to eat. Suzuki stays by, helping. There is plenteous rice, and stewed fish floating in a sweetish sauce, and a special dish of rice into which eggs have been broken raw. Of course, there is tea in tiny cups, and red, sour "sweetmeats" and sugar. It was not bad, any of it, as a novelty; and the chopsticks are easy to use. But there is one frequent article of diet to which I must really pay my respects,—a sort of pickled radish, known as *daikon*. It has the odor of an ancient egg, tastes worse than it smells, and is just about as nutritious as a corn-stalk. With more force than elegance, perhaps, it may be truthfully described as preserved stink. Yet it is a favorite with the Japanese palate. One of the dishes most acceptable to alien taste is *unagi-meshi*, which consists of fried eels in boiled rice, flavored with the sweetish sauce that is used for almost everything. A new dish at Suzuki's was whale's meat. It looked and tasted like beef, being somewhat redder and more pungent. Karatsu is a great fish market; strange ogling monsters they showed me in the stalls. Some of the daintiest fish is served raw. One dips

The Mid-day Meal

HOME LIFE

it in soy, and it is palatable. Other dishes, like the soups and stewed chicken, are not unlike your own; then there is the rice, and the tea. But of all of it one tires in three days.

They were very kind to me,—painstaking to please, yet without affectation. Is not that true hospitality? Friends of the family came to call on me, and we played *Gomoku-narabe*,—vulgarly known here as Go-bang. Most graciously did they feign defeat; most untruthfully praise the Westerner's skill, who is as naught before them. Then Suzuki takes up the bow again, and we go to the seashore to shoot. Their archery is all hedged about with occult rules; if the bow is not held just *so*, and the feather cradled in the hand like *this*, truly there is no doing! So I cannot do. In the evening they have a noble lady come in to play the *koto*, that most musical of all Japanese instruments,—a sort of lyre,—but why will she sing? Many apologies and excuses at first, but when once started, there is no stopping her (humanity the same the world over),—and her voice like a rusty lawn-mower! Suzuki could not wink at me, being a Japanese, but he looked very sage, and said in an aside, that " she does like the singing of herself." Her boy, a lad of ten, they called the Judge, because of his droll soberness.

The Judge and his mother went home, and they put me to bed. First came the young women of the family, to pull out the wadded bedclothes from the closets and spread them on the floor. Whenever they entered, Suzuki apologized for the fool-women being in my presence; and here, indeed, was a surety of Orientalism. Apologizing for the ladies! This is the land where one of the common proverbs runs, " Though a woman bear you seven sons, trust her not." Yet they do trust her to make the beds, the gawky men sitting helpless. For my especial comfort an improvised baggish pillow was thoughtfully provided, instead of the usual "head-rest," which looks like a little wooden anvil and feels like the block of an executioner. Only in the women did I see any signs of devoutness. Morning and evening the mother uncovered a gilded shrine in the wall, filled with bronze lotus-leaves sheltering a Buddha; twice a day she opened this sacred place, clapped her hands, struck silvery notes on a hanging bell-cup near the shrine, and made offerings of new tea and smoking rice, while

HOME LIFE

her son blushed. Better any religion than none, say I—better old Japan than young, if irreligious. There is an ancient motto on the wall of that pagan home which reads, "Uprightness putteth a hundred devils to flight."

It was on the second evening they summoned courage, after a family council, to ask me to a bath. Vague rumors had reached them of strange Western prudery, yet to omit this daily offer would be a breach of "uprightness," and righteousness prevailed. No doubt there was relief when I declined, and all could go trooping singly to the family ablution, beginning with the eldest, and so down. Afterwards a momentous question was put to me. Said the curious elder brother: "Whereas they say that Westerners go wearing their clothes into the bath, is it not so?" They think it inexplicable that we should wear clothing so constantly; and, never seeing us without it, draw inferences.

Their bath-tubs are often placed in a corner of the little front yard, entirely unconcealed. Any day you may see a father and his children snugly ensconced in their wooden tub, only their red, perspiring heads showing above the water-line, the charcoal boiler within the tub maintaining a degree

JAPAN TO-DAY

of heat that we could not for a moment endure. Bath-houses for men and women alike open blandly on the public streets. They deem it no immodesty to expose the body for purposes of utility, but, on the other hand, express surprise at the apparently useless *décolleté* styles of Western women.

Now, the best thing about that visit to Suzuki's house I cannot describe. A strange feeling came to me many times whilst in that home. It was a feeling of reminiscence. Among all those peculiar customs and surroundings—when eating whale, or listening to the *koto*—my mind was filled with the flavor of an American country hospitality. At times it was hard to shake off the impression that I was home again, in the Carolina country, among the whole-souled farmers there. For humanity is the same the world over, and I had caught a glimpse of it in Japan; not of their etiquette, mind you, or their art, but of something deeper. Yet it was the one only chance of years. A few days later, back in school again, Suzuki furtively approached and said: "Teacher, please do not say to the boys that you made me a visit." He had been ashamed of his mother's religion before the foreigner;

HOME LIFE

he was ashamed before the boys of his own humanity.

There is no home life without children. During the years of my Japanese sojourn I found constant delight and interest in the little brown babies of the Orient. Many are the children's festivals observed in that frolicsome land; and infinite pains are taken, which become reciprocal pleasures, to make the little ones happy. In beautiful Nikkō, on the morning of the first of July, I awoke to find a gay, fluttering world come suddenly to birth with the sunrise: as though it had rained flags and peppermints; as though some jolly Saint Nicholas had toyed with the world in midsummer. In wonder, I asked a young Japanese friend the reason why those long sprigs of bamboo are decorated with strips and streamers of gay colored paper, bedecking almost every house in sight, and presenting a most pleasing appearance. He tells me it is the feast of Amanogawa. Up there near the Milky Way, which is really "the heavenly river,"—there, on either bank of the wide silvery river, there dwell a separated lover and his mate. He

JAPAN TO-DAY

is a shepherd, and she is a weaving-girl; he is a star in Aquila, she is the mild star Vega. Only in one night of all the long and lonesome year can lover and mate be united; and that is the last night in June. So this morning the world is alive with bright poems, verses of congratulation lifted by these gracious, sentimental people of the East, lifted on sprigs of the waving bamboo to comfort those far lonely lovers of the air. For the weaving-girl is kept always busy at her loom, weaving garments for the innumerable children of the stars, and her lover, far across the silvery river, can come to her but once in the year. Since the stars first sang together, they have loved; and they will love till the stars grow old.

Amid this atmosphere of poetry and world-old romance, hedged in by charming ceremonial and enlivened by frequent festive jollity, the little master of the East journeys on the road to manhood. Bright-eyed, rosy little tonsured monk, wrapped in his robes of rustling silk, borne on the bending back of a slightly older brother, a tot atop of a toddler — the Japanese world seems especially made for him, and Japan is the children's paradise.

The Empress in Western Dress

HOME LIFE

That is what many travellers have called Japan, where so much is done to amuse the little ones, whose parents, indeed, are childlike in many of their fancies. And yet Japan is not a children's paradise in every sense. Loud cries were heard, one day, from the house of our Nikkō neighbor. Looking down from our upper piazza, one could see a mother applying the moxa to the back of one of her children, a boy about seven years old, who was kicking and screaming most lustily. But he was scarcely to be blamed for crying. Moxa is the Japanese name for the plant that we commonly call mugwort. When a child is naughty, or when its mother wishes to ward off the evil spirits, or to cure it of some disease, she rolls the mugwort up into a fierce little cone, which she sticks to the child's tender body and forthwith sets on fire! It leaves a scar that lasts throughout life. Sometimes a coolie's body is pretty well covered with these scars of the terrible moxa. But the practice is now on the wane.

While walking through the grounds of one of the beautiful Nikkō temples, I once met a real child-princess. She is one of the Emperor's daughters—a wee thing, not more than five years old—spending the sum-

JAPAN TO-DAY

mer in a royal house here near the tombs of her ancestors. Noblemen and court ladies encompassed her; when I saw her, two or three grown people were fanning hard enough to blow her away, it would seem, and waiting on her every movement. Of course my friend and I took off our hats in her presence; and she, in turn, stared very hard at the foreigners.

The children seem exceedingly free and happy—playing in the dirt, romping through the road, much as our children at home. Their minds do not seem quite so active, perhaps; but to make up for this, their bodies are surprisingly supple. You should see even the very little ones racing over a hill or beside a sleepy lake! I am sure you could not keep up with them.

Baby-carriages are not often seen. Baby is oftener carried on his sister's or his brother's back, in a kind of bag, though frequently he is supported only by the strong arms of his nurse, which reach around and clasp him safely from behind. Sometimes you see a child not more than four years old carrying a still smaller baby in this way. Such a system of nursing has its disadvantages; for the baby's head lolls back until the

HOME LIFE

cruel sun shines straight down and hurts his eyes, perhaps for life; while the nurse is apt to become stoop-shouldered from the weight so constantly borne.

You would surely feel like laughing could you see the way his mother fixes baby's hair, when he gets old enough to have any. There are several fashions in hair-dressing, but the favorite way is to shave a round spot, the size of a small saucer, on top of the little fellow's head. This makes him look exactly as though he were bald; but then he doesn't seem to mind it.

His hair is always black or brown. The Japanese think it very strange that many of us foreigners should have light hair. There is a young American blonde out there whom they call "Miss Golden Hair," but whether they admire her style of beauty is hard to say. Probably they prefer the darker locks of their own familiar folk.

"Do the Japanese babies have any Sunday-school?" Yes, some of them have. Those that have Christian parents go on Sunday mornings, just as our children do, to the chapel where they are taught about the Wonderful Child of Nazareth. But millions of them have never heard of the manger of

JAPAN TO-DAY

Bethlehem, so that their growing hearts are taught to worship idols that cannot love them in return. In almost every Buddhist temple you will find a figure cut out of senseless stone, whither the mothers bring their sickly little ones, that they may be healed. One of the saddest sights I have seen in Japan was when I saw these pale, great-eyed children caressing a stone idol whose face had been worn quite round and smooth by weakly hands that hoped to be thus made strong.

An American child has asked me how the Japanese worship their gods. They pray, after having thrown some money to the idols that they may be induced to listen. Kneeling humbly at an altar, with bowed heads and clasped hands, they mutter prayer after prayer, and then depart. In Osaka you may see a peculiar kind of praying going on —prayer for the dead. The people pay the priest to write the name of the departed one upon a sort of paper, which they cast into a pool that is supposed to flow from heaven. Of course this is all very well for the priests, who get all of the money. These priests themselves are sometimes very diligent in prayer. They read the petition aloud from a book as rapidly as they can, whilst knocking

HOME LIFE

a block all the while with a very shrill-voiced little wooden hammer. Perhaps they do this to keep the god awake, or else to keep time to their own sing-song words. I stood one day for a long time watching a boy-priest praying thus earnestly, seated as he was flat on the floor of his temple, his head shaved, the perspiration dripping from his face. As I walked away through the beautiful grove, there still came ringing out the ceaseless *click, click, click* of the little hammer, until I was out of hearing distance. Each temple is provided with a large, sweet-toned bell, which is rung at certain hours to remind the people of their duteous worship. Every night near eleven o'clock, when all other sounds are stilled, I could always hear the solemn notes of a temple bell near by, rung in praise of a god that cannot hear it.

Some one has asked me whether the children can sing. They cannot sing as ours do; the Japanese are scarcely a musical people. In the Sunday-schools, the children learn the same tunes that we know; but they have little music of their own. If you were to hear even what they have, you would not call it music. It is noise. My servant's little boy had a foreign accordeon, of which he is very fond, much to my deep regret. The most popular native instrument is a guitar-like contrivance known as a *samisen*. I have laughed until the tears came, listening to a man playing his *samisen* by moonlight, while he was grunting out, in the most ridiculous nasal voice, a mournful ditty without any tune whatsoever. A Japanese girl may be pretty until you hear her sing, but then the beauty vanishes.

During three days in the spring comes the Tsukiji feast of Inari, the rice god, or fox deity. Inari is commonly represented as a very fat, jolly old fellow, sitting on his bags of rice. The Japanese are very fond of him, since rice is their chief dependence. So his festival is a great season. Almost every hour in the day a long and noisy procession would pass my house. In front was a man carrying two small blocks of wood, which he would click together now and then, as a signal for the procession to move or halt. Behind him came men dressed fantastically,—some of them with false red noses a foot long; others riding funny make-believe horses, and yet others, with painted faces, robed in long white gowns and wearing tall black hats. After these

HOME LIFE

came two long lines of children, pulling, by ropes, a tall wooden car, all decorated with flags and gay paper ornaments. On top of this car sat men, blowing fifes and beating drums and ringing bells. The children were shouting and the babies were crying, so that altogether those three days were somewhat wearisome to the flesh.

There are festivals and festivals galore. There are the festivals of New Year, which almost every traveller's diary has described; a feast in April to commemorate the birth of Buddha; a picturesque lantern-festival in midsummer; a festival of Good-Luck in early autumn; several Shintō festivals in November, and local feasts too numerous to mention. But for the children, the two supreme events of all the year are the girls' festival, in March, and that of the boys, in May. The former is also called "the feast of dolls;" for on the third of March all the doll-shops in all the cities are decked out in such fashion as to set the little ones fairly agog with delight. The Japanese excel in doll-making. We rarely see, in this country, any but the cheaper grades of their work. In Japan I have been deceived by the marvellous life-likeness of the little "men-images,"

JAPAN TO-DAY

taking them to be real children. So imagine a doll-festival day in Japan! All of the toy-shops are filled with tiny models of all sorts of people and things, the whole Japanese world in miniature. It is the day of the girls' rejoicing.

But Japan wears its most picturesque aspect during the boys' festival, in May. The carp is the chosen symbol of boyhood, because he swims upstream against all manner of obstacles, resolved at all cost of strenuousness to make his own way in the world. So the people make great toy carps of paper, tough and fibrous, with a large hoop at the mouth, and a much smaller hoop at the tail. Then they hoist these great fish to the top of flagstaffs, one for the roof of each house, and the wind goes in at the mouth and fills out the sides of the carp to lifelike proportions, and they swim and wriggle and dart through the air, for all the world as though the ocean were above us. I doubt whether the earth holds a more picturesque spectacle than Japan affords on the fifth of every May.

We may pause a moment longer with the children to hear the story they are taught concerning the creation of the world,—which

HOME LIFE

means Japan. The beautiful islands were made by the gods themselves, two of whom came down to live there, becoming the progenitors of the present inhabitants, who are thus the "sons of heaven," as they literally call their Emperors to this day. The advent story of these divine progenitors is certainly interesting, and suggestive of several things. Izanagi the god and Izanami the goddess each took a walk around the borders of the newly-created realm, going in opposite directions. At length they met. Instantly Izanami exclaimed, "Oh, what a beautiful man!" But Izanagi was disappointed that a woman should precede him in anything, even in the matter of flattering speech; so this literal lord of creation commanded that they walk around the islands again, and that the goddess keep silent upon their meeting, thus giving him his divine right of precedence. Izanami meekly obeyed him, and when next they met she held her nimble tongue, while her liege lord sluggishly ejaculated, "Oh, what a beautiful woman!"

Of course, they lived happily ever afterwards. But this story is unintentionally suggestive of several conclusions, all of which happen to be true. The Japanese woman is

JAPAN TO-DAY

brighter by nature than the average Japanese man. But the man, by the rule of brute force, compels her to give way before him,— then speaks the woman's speech after her. So Eve has her way after all! Japan has been for ages preëminent in the subjection of woman. But there, as elsewhere, the truth is that "the hand that rocks the cradle rules the world."

This leads me to speak of those Japanese home-makers, the mothers, the wives, the women. Yet I believe I know less about them than of any other class of the people. Indeed, it is extremely hazardous to speak with assurance of the characteristics of any of the people. Missionaries that have spent long years in Japan are often unwilling to risk any definite opinions as to the real character of the people; and when they do venture to express their opinions, some one else with equal or superior experience is likely to think just the opposite. Nevertheless, for one who keeps his eyes wide open, there are many opportunities for observing at least the surface characteristics of the native life; and so, perhaps, I shall be able to write some-

Japanese Girls and Women

HOME LIFE

what of the Japanese women, not as they necessarily are, but as they appear to me to be.

To begin with that which is easiest, let me try to sketch how they look. They are considerably smaller than Americans, and fashion ordains that they stoop. Their complexion is neither yellow nor brown, but something between the two—a dusky sort of fairness that is by no means unattractive. Almost without exception—and I saw no exceptions—they have luxuriant growths of very dark-brown or else a jet-black hair. It is wonderful to see how some of them manage to arrange their crown of glory. The hair is smeared with some unguent that makes it glossy and smooth, and then it is gracefully rolled into outstanding convolutions, whereon gay ornaments are fastened. Others patronize different styles of arrangement, but all are equally interesting to the new-comer. It is no uncommon thing for a woman invalid to cut off all of her beautiful hair and send it to a temple in fulfilment of a vow made so to do if the patron divinity would but spare the life. I have often seen these votive offerings suspended at the entrance to some Buddhist temple, to which

JAPAN TO-DAY

women flock by multitudes in seemingly earnest prayer.

It would be unfair to leave their complexions where I did. Often a healthy, brilliant rosiness creeps athwart the dusky cheek, and makes a Japanese almost beautiful. I have, however, seen but one woman that I should term a genuine beauty. She had the warm, dreamy eyes that adorn all her sisters; her complexion was perfect in a brunette way; her nose straight, her mouth full but refined, her figure slender, and her hands exquisitely delicate. My entrancement was somewhat dispelled when she pulled out a tiny pipe and began to smoke, as almost all Japanese women are said to do.

As to the kind of clothes the women wear, the main garment consists in a loose robe with flowing sleeves. The quality of the clothes varies, of course, according to the importance of the occasion. Sometimes it is of silk, beautifully decorated. The whole garment is bound to the waist by a wide silk sash, which is tied behind into an enormous bow, sometimes reaching almost to the neck.

The Japanese women, like so many Americans, often succeed in spoiling their complexions by the undue use of cosmetics. Un-

HOME LIFE

like Americans, however, no attempt is made at concealment in this regard. A very white rice-powder is bestowed bounteously upon the soft skin, and a touch of scarlet paint is dabbed into the centre of the lower lip.

But I am filling in my sketch with a description of how our sisters look, and have but little space left to tell you how they act. Before leaving the subject, however, I must not omit to mention the unfortunately prominent custom of blacking the teeth, still prevalent among married women, but said to be dying out. Sound teeth of glistening whiteness are thus often converted into hideous semblances of decay.

One of the first points that attracted my attention in the Japanese woman is the universal sweetness of her voice in conversation. It is soft, mellow, flute-like. The same cannot be said of the voice in song; it then seems transformed by some evil influence into the flat squawk of a duck. At the commencements of the mission schools I often listened to the voices as trained after foreign models. The flatness, the lack of real music, was still most sadly apparent; and I particularly noted a certain lifelessness in the singing, so strongly in contrast with the liveliness of

JAPAN TO-DAY

American girls under similar circumstances. By the way, one does not fully appreciate American girls until they are out of sight. "Blessings brighten as they take their flight."

Yet I would not have it understood that Japanese women are habitually lifeless. They are just the reverse in ordinary intercourse. Their good nature and merriness are irresistible. Even old women, with silvered hair, are gay and almost "jolly." They crack jokes with you sometimes at a tea-house, but their levity is withal so dignified and refined that one cannot take exception to it on the ground of familiarity.

The chief attraction of the Japanese woman, as I have already hinted, lies in her gentleness. She knows how to spank the baby when he needs it, but this is one of those exceptions that prove the rule. She is seemingly tender with her child, though sometimes she does not scruple to extinguish its new-born life, reasoning that it is better the child should die than to endure a life of hardship. Sad instances of this nature occurred frequently during my sojourn. But, viewed in one light, this is an additional proof of gentleness, sadly misdirected

HOME LIFE

though it be. Think how the murdering mother's heart must bleed as she darkens that tiny spark of life; and yet she chooses this personal suffering in order to save her child, as she supposes—for the family may be in deepest poverty, with already many hungry little mouths crying for their scant supplies of food.

And now I shall but dimly indicate the dark background of the picture I have so unably sketched. The portrait would not be true should I quite leave out the gloom. These gentle, patient souls, whose lives are often uncomplainingly given to a service of the most exacting kind; who submit obediently to the harsh demands of father, or brother, or husband; they have not learned the same high ideal of womanly purity and honor that is so warmly cherished in the hearts of those that love the Virgin's Son. Whilst some are pure and true, many more, outwardly sweet and refined, are inwardly unclean. Some missionaries that have spent long years in the country deny that the Japanese, as a nation, have any conception of chastity. I adjudge this a harsh and hazardous assertion. But it is true that the masses of women and men alike are ignorant of

JAPAN TO-DAY

those principles of right that animate the ambition of the Christian. And how can it be otherwise, seeing they know not the source of purity and peace?

Confucianism, which moulds the morals of Japan as well as of China, conceives of womanhood with infinite contempt. An eminent Japanese Confucianist, in his famous treatise on "The Whole Duty of Woman," delights in deliverances such as these:

"The five worst maladies that afflict the female mind are: indocility, discontent, slander, jealousy, and silliness. Without any doubt, these five maladies infest seven or eight out of every ten women, and it is from these that arises the inferiority of women to men. The worst of them all, and the parent of the other four, is silliness. Woman's nature, in comparison with man's, is as the shadow to the sunlight. Hence, as viewed from the standard of man's nature, the foolishness of woman fails to understand the duties that lie before her very eyes, perceives not the actions that will bring down blame upon her own head, and comprehends not even the things that will bring down calamities on the heads of her husband and children. Such is the stupidity of her character

HOME LIFE

that it is incumbent on her, in every particular, to distrust herself and to obey her husband."

The teachings of Confucius, as recorded by this same disciple, state these "Seven Reasons for Divorce:"

"1. A woman shall be divorced for disobedience to her father-in-law or mother-in-law.

"2. A woman shall be divorced if she fail to bear children, the reason for this rule being that women are sought in marriage for the purpose of giving men posterity.

"3. Lewdness is a reason for divorce.

"4. Jealousy is a reason for divorce.

"5. Leprosy, or any like foul disease, is a reason for divorce.

"6. A woman shall be divorced, who, by talking over much and prattling disrespectfully, disturbs the harmony of kinsmen and brings trouble on her household.

"7. Stealing is a reason for divorce."

It is little wonder that the disciples of such teaching hold women in unutterable contempt. Nor is it easy to disabuse the minds of Christian converts, of this ingrained and shameful prejudice. It fell to my lot to witness the courtship of a young Christian minister. He came shamefacedly and asked that an older friend be permitted to go find a wife for him. So the elderly "go-between" went on a tour of investigation up the river, in search of a Christian wife. On his return he reported to the groom-elect that he had found two sisters, and asked which one of them was preferred. The young man not unnaturally replied that on general principles he would choose the younger. But the old man, on further consideration of the question, decided that the elder girl would be the more desirable.

"Oh, all right," said the complaisant and contemptuous groom; "it's a matter of indifference to me."

So the older man went on a second journey up the river, and this time he brought the happy damsel back with him—the Japanese bride being always brought for marriage to the house of her lordly husband. The Christian form of wedding was, of course, requested, but the bridegroom wanted the ceremony to be somewhat seriously modified.

"Teacher," said he to me, "kindly condescend to deign that I be not compelled to stand side by side with a woman before spectators."

A Wedding in Old Japan

HOME LIFE

I told him that he would have to stand beside his wife, both then and forever thereafter.

"Then, at least," he pleaded, "at least honorably deign to let it be so that I shall not have to touch her hand!"

I told him that if it were to be a Christian ceremony it would have to be a Christian ceremony. But I shall never forget how that martyred bridegroom, at the fateful words, "Join your right hands," actually clenched his teeth, and shut his eyes fast, and wheeled towards his humble bride with his hand stuck out as though to the stroke of an axe!

There was in Tōkyō a native Christian pastor who asked permission of his missionary employers to come to America for study. They were about to accede to his request, when it occurred to some one to inquire how he intended to obtain the means. Imagine the amazement of his questioners when he replied that it was his intention to secure the money by renting out his wife to a temporary life of shame! "Morality" still meant to him little more than the "filialism" of a subordinate to a superior authority; and the obedience of his wife to her hus-

JAPAN TO-DAY

band's behest would thus have been an act of "righteousness."

The modern education of women has not kept pace with the general educational scheme. Mr. Lewis points out that after twenty years of experience the reports of the educational bureau showed that while seventy-nine per cent. of the boys of school age were under instruction, there were only forty-seven per cent. of the girls. The department took a great step forward in the year 1890, however, when an official report declared that "female education is the source from which general education should be diffused over the whole country;" while the establishment, in 1901, of an independent Women's University marked a great advance in the training of women. Hitherto, as has been shown, woman was regarded as but a toy and slave. Her domestic duties engrossed all of her time, and they were of the most menial order. When she appeared socially, it was always in the position of an inferior. But Japan is reaching out towards the light.

If it be true, as our beloved "Autocrat" so wisely said, that a man's education must begin with his grandfather, then it is at least

Good-night!

HOME LIFE

equally true that a nation cannot be spiritually born in a day. The Japanese really have no such word as "home." Until we can teach them, by long and patient effort, the practical meaning of that holy word, they cannot have entered the spiritual fellowship of Christian nations. But just as the Gospel in days of old slowly but surely uplifted the nations of Europe by teaching the sanctity of childhood, the purity of womanhood, and the manliness of manhood, so at length the same uplifting power will bring like blessings to Japan.

V

THE AWFUL JAPANESE LANGUAGE

¶ What it is Not—Honorifics—Chinese Complications—The Blunders of Beginners—"Why I Study English"

V

THE AWFUL JAPANESE LANGUAGE

MARK TWAIN has never attempted Japanese, else he would never have written his essay on "The Awful German Language." The sturdy speech of the Teutons, complicated as it is in its constructions, cumbersome in its verbal forms, and perplexing in its genders, is simple by the side of *Nihon-Go*. While it is almost true, as Mr. Clemens asserts, that there are more exceptions to some German rules of grammar than correspondents, it is certainly true that the German language is a *system*, with a well-articulated skeleton and a logical growth of compact flesh; but colloquial Japanese is a dislocated heap of bones waiting for an anatomist to set them in place. The anatomist has not yet been found. Consequently the language sadly lacks system. It is dislocated and often illogical. Many of its growths, and even elements, are as yet quite unexplained. It is hard.

Of course I speak from an Occidental

stand-point, for I could not well speak otherwise. It may be that, to an Oriental, the language in question is symmetrical and systematic; but I doubt it. Certain it is that to one whose whole mental structure and training seems antipodal to Eastern ways of thought, this mass of unruly words is little else than a mass.

But let us to our task. I shall not presume to tell what the Japanese language is, but rather what it is not. To compare Japanese, then, with those languages usually embraced in a college curriculum, and to note its points of disagreement with them, it is remarkable in the first place that the Japanese language ignores both number and gender. The verb is always the same, whether as predicate for the first, or second, or third persons. *Shokusuru* means I eat, you eat, he or she eats, we eat, and they eat. It is as unchangeable as the notorious laws of the Medes and Persians. It does not recognize personality; it has no person. If I happen to be in a hurry, and run, the action is expressed by the verb *hashiru;* and if I wish to speak of a dog exercising himself in the same manner, it is done by saying *hashiru*. The simple, indefinite form *run*, expresses both meanings,

THE LANGUAGE

extending also to the plural, as indicated in the preceding example of the verb eat.

It is bad enough for the verb to be so impersonal and so numberless, but the deficiency is the more apparent in the noun itself. *Inu* means either dog or dogs; *bōshi* may denote one hat or a dozen. The word for the coin *yen*, which corresponds to our dollar, does not vary to denote multiplication—this task is left to the numeral adjectives. Only where it is absolutely necessary are words suffixed to signify plurality; in all other cases one must judge from the context whether the subject be single or otherwise. And so it is with gender.

This disregard of personality naturally embraces a contempt for personal pronouns, so freely used in English. Only in cases of special emphasis or antithesis is the reluctant pronoun employed. Thus the single word *kaerimashita* will mean "I have come back," or "*he, we, she, you, it, they* came back," according to the previous drift of conversation. A Japanese will often discourse for half an hour without using a single personal pronoun.

There are no declensions in this queer language; neither is there any article. It is, in fact, maintained by one of the leading grammarians that there are properly but two parts of speech, the verb and the noun. He declares that the particles or post-positions and suffixes, which take the place of our prepositions, conjunctions, and conjugational terminations, were themselves originally fragments of nouns and verbs. The pronoun and numeral are simply nouns. The true adjective (including the adverb) is a sort of neuter verb. "Altogether, our grammatical categories do not fit the Japanese language well."

The term "post-position" is foreign to English grammar, but is properly employed to designate the Japanese particle corresponding to our preposition; for the people, who really seem perverse in their habit of acting contrariwise to us, place this particle after the noun, instead of before it. There is no stable form for the arrangement of a sentence, as in English; consequently a separate post-position is required to show each distinct case relation. Thus *ga* or *wa* is the sign of the nominative; *wo*, placed after its noun, of course, like all the rest, denotes the objective or accusative; and *no* the possessive. These particles are very numerous and,

THE LANGUAGE

to make the matter worse, they have various synonyms.

The statement was just made that Japanese has no declensions, and yet there are adjective terminations, varying to express case relation, that approximate such a definition. This is an additional source of annoyance and perplexity to the student, who, for instance, in using the word "white," must vary it, accordingly as it is used as an attribute, predicate, or stem, into *shiroi, shiroku,* or *shiro*.

Another characteristic of Japanese is its full and complicated system of honorifics. Different forms are used to express different degrees of politeness and respect, to which custom conformity is necessary if one would appear at all well-bred or educated. Honorifics are used in speaking of the actions or possessions of the person addressed, while depreciatory or humble forms are employed in speaking of one's self. In other words, what we should style the first person is self-depreciatory, and the second person is complimentary. In speaking of others, honorifics are used if the person spoken of is superior in rank to the person spoken to, or if he is present, and, though not a superior, at least an equal, or assumed to be so for courtesy's sake. As stated, there are also gradations in the use of these honorific terms, according to the greater or less respect meant to be shown the person spoken to or of. These idioms affect not only the vocabulary, but the very grammar itself. It is saturated with them.

Several chapters of this book would be necessary in order to give some adequate idea of the perverse grammatical constructions. But that would be outside the purpose of this sketch, which purports to show only what the language is *not*, when contrasted with the English. Perhaps this cannot better be done than by rendering a few simple phrases into their exact Japanese equivalents, as regards construction. Thus, "Please excuse me," becomes "August excuse deign;" "Go slowly," "Augustly leisurely going deign to be;" "Sit down a moment," "A little honorably hip-suspending deign;" "I feel bad," "Bodily state bad is;" "Please tell me," "Causing-to-hear condescend;" "Good-evening," "This night as-for;" "Good-morning," "Honorable earliness is."

From these examples, two conclusions may easily be drawn: first, that honorifics com-

THE LANGUAGE

plicate the language almost hopelessly, and secondly, that it is impossible to translate English literally into Japanese. The English phrase must first be contemplated from a Japanese point of view, and this reclothed expression then translated into its equivalents.

By this time the reader is doubtless prepared for anything. He will therefore not be surprised upon learning that the above remarks apply to but half of the Japanese language, which is distinctly divided into two languages, the spoken and the written. The latter has a different grammar from that of the spoken language, and employs to some extent a different vocabulary. Moreover, its modes of visible expression are extremely difficult of comprehension and manipulation, since it employs no less than a half-dozen alphabets of seventy-two letters each, besides necessitating a scholarly knowledge of Chinese. For Chinese has established itself, so to speak, as the Latin and Greek of Japan, with this difference, that it lends its thousands of written signs bodily. The two languages are wedded, without the remotest prospect of possible divorce. China supplies to Japan names for almost all the new implements, sciences, and ideas, that are being introduced from the West. Moreover, this influx of Chinese terms is by no means in its inception. It has been in order for more than a millenium, and its final effect is to discredit the original Japanese equivalents, so that a foreigner that wishes to be considered an elegant speaker should gradually accustom himself to employ Chinese words very freely, except when addressing uneducated persons.

In some instances the interlocking of the two languages produces a seemingly needless perplexity, as in the case of numerals. Only Chinese numerals are used above the number ten, but below that the two forms exist side by side, and one must be chosen or rejected according to the etymological history of the word it governs. One day I employed a Japanese numeral instead of a Chinese, quite ignorantly, of course, and for the reason that it was easier to remember. I noticed a restrained smile pass over the faces of two or three that heard me, and subsequently learned that my mistake was about the equivalent of such an English barbarism as one would commit in speaking of a herd of birds!

It is not easy to store the memory with

THE LANGUAGE

strange words and their correct pronunciation. To illustrate: I have committed that irritating blunder of washing my face in soapy water without a towel near at hand. With eyes tight shut, I grope for the towel-rack, and grope in vain, for there is nothing on it. Toku San, the servant, is called, and I congratulate myself on my good memory in recalling the word for towel, which I enounce in a commanding tone. Toku San, ejaculating an assentive "*Hai,*" hastens away. Meanwhile my eyes are smarting, and the water is trickling down my back. Toku San returns; the misery is over! Eagerly I reach out towards him, without daring to raise those leaky lids, and finally clutch—a pin-cushion!

On another occasion, at a tea-house, I tried to ask for a plate, but succeeded only in making the landlady believe that I was hungry for monkey,—which did not seem in the least to surprise her, by the way, as she had evidently learned that in the case of "the hairy foreigner" there is no accounting for tastes. The infinitesimal variation of certain vowel quantities is accountable for ludicrous mistakes. I never did learn the difference between a persimmon and an oyster, and I

JAPAN TO-DAY

gravely doubt whether anybody else has. But this is not so vital a matter as that which vexed a missionary friend of mine. Ambitious to preach as soon as possible, he delivered one night a learned and eloquent discourse on the attributes of God, after he had been in the country six months. The faces of his hearers speedily assumed an expression of mystified interest. This interest rapidly deepened into something approaching awe. But their awe presently gave way to laughter, hilarious, uproarious, and disconcerting, as it dawned upon them that the missionary was not talking about "turtles" at all, but was trying to talk about God. The two words being very similar to an untrained ear, he had been insisting that Turtles created the world, and in them we live, and move, and have our being!

Another missionary once acquitted himself with a feeling of great satisfaction. This feeling was intensified as a dignified and interested listener came forward with words of gratified comment. But the sensations of the preacher may be better imagined than described as his appreciative auditor continued:

"Truly, as for the honorable sermon, it was greatly interesting. I listened to it well.

THE LANGUAGE

If you ask why, it was the first time I ever heard a discourse in the English tongue. And how much your language is like the language of Japan!"

Space fails me to tell of the invalid missionary who asked his startled servant for a bath of molasses instead of a bath of rain water; or of the cannibal missionary who said that "To-day for the first time I ate a baby," instead of, "To-day for the first time I ate bamboo."

Sufficient instances have been cited to justify the remark of the first great missionary to Japan, Francis Xavier, who in the sixteenth century expressed the emphatic conviction that the language of the natives was clearly an invention of the devil to prevent the preaching of the Christian faith. He might have added with equal justification that it seems to be maliciously designed for preventing the exercise of Christian works on the part of those who learn it; for it is very hard even for a missionary to study Japanese and at the same time refrain his lips that they speak no guile—in forcible English expletives, for the strongest Japanese swear-word is "That!" How do I wish that those beautiful rumors were true, and

JAPAN TO-DAY

the Chinese ideographs supplanted by the Roman alphabet! How vividly do I recall the slow perspiring hours spent in poring over ponderous dictionaries and chaotic grammars! A grammar and a dictionary are beside me, and another dictionary is in my lap. One is Japanese, the other Chinese. They tell me that when I have learned about four thousand of the sixty-odd thousand Chinese characters I shall be prepared to learn something about the literary language. Usually, the Chinese character has its Japanese equivalents printed by its side; but sometimes these are omitted, and frequently the Japanese word cannot be found at all without recourse to the Chinese. So the proper Chinese ideograph is finally traced to its hidden lair through a laborious process of interlocking indexes of radicals. Once found, however, you have before you only the English meaning, for the Japanese pronunciation of the ideograph is sure to be very different from the original, being susceptible, indeed, of three or four different readings according to circumstances. You must wait until your teacher comes to tell you what to call it. This mild-mannered and obsequious individual comes once a day, five days in the

THE LANGUAGE

week, and stays two hours or more each visit. He means well, but you must be continually teaching him how to teach you. Moreover, his incorrigible politeness often prevents him from telling you of your mistakes, and sometimes even leads him to speak "pidgin"-Japanese, in order to adapt himself to your benighted understanding. Consequently much of your precious time is wasted in unlearning what was wrongly learned. The teacher usually proceeds upon the hypothesis that a foreigner cannot learn Japanese any way, and that the most the teacher may hope to do is to persuade him that he can. This kindly endeavor almost always fails.

There are, however, delicious compensations. The inflated youths of the Island Empire are ambitious to learn "the Engliss," with motives that will be illuminated presently. Their vanity prompts them to a ceaseless display of their ignorance. It is manna to a hungry soul to hear them flounder through a simple English phrase. A missionary was waiting at a railway station. A sauntering student became imbued with the double desire of ascertaining the alien's destination and of airing his speaking acquaintance with an alien tongue. So he struck a soldierly attitude before my overawed friend, and shouted forth the stentorian question,—

"What you go?"

My avengeful friend said to him, in soothing tones,—

"Suppose you try that over again."

The student retired into privacy, lost himself in laborious thought for about ten minutes, and then renewed the charge.

"You go what?" he thundered.

The missionary collapsed.

I once saw an elderly foreigner lose his temper with an obstreperous coolie. It is said that in moments of profound self-abandonment the stranger in a strange land, however long his residence, will recur to the language of youth. At any rate, in this particular instance the elderly and pious gentleman backed the coolie up against a wall, clutched him where the lapel of his coat would have been had he worn any, and administered in classical but vigorous English a choice dissertation calculated to inculcate a higher standard of ethical ideals. The coolie of necessity missed the form of this eloquent address, being absolutely ignorant of English; but its spirit was by no means lost upon him. He began to tremble vio-

THE LANGUAGE

lently; jerked his head continually in wild nods of assent to all that was going forward; and finally fell to his knees in abject terror, seized the irate orator about the legs, and piteously begged for mercy. It gives one renewed confidence and self-respect to see a thing like that.

I beg you to notice some of the English signs that adorn the streets for the seduction of the shopping globe-trotter. The shopkeepers of Japan, like the students, are anxious to show all they know about our language—and succeed. Here is a sign which denotes the presence of a

LADIES CLOTHS TAILER.

Presumably the gentleman is a seamstress. Another knight of the needle is somewhat more ambitious, with his alluring announcement:

TAILOR NATIVE GOUNTRY, DRAPER, MILLINER
& LADIES OUTFATTER, THE RIBBONS,
THE LACES, THE VEILS, THE
FEELINGS.

Here a dry-goods house gravely assures us, in large letters, that

DO NOT BE CHEAPEN, NO BUY,

JAPAN TO-DAY

while another mystifies with the promise,

EUROPEAN MONKEY JACKET MAKE FOR THE JAPANESE.

Here we are offered at a low price,

THE IMPROVED MILK.

Yonder is a
TIME PIECE SNOP,
TO SELL THE INSURABLE WATCH.

Over there is a

CARVER & GILDER FOR SALE,

while above an excellent restaurant gleams the brutally humble announcement,

A GROG SHOP, A POT HOUSE.

Now, I abominate the personal use of the razor. And I was so often allured, in the early days, by the frequent signs of "BABER SOP" and "THE BABER," that one day my combined curiosity and laziness got the better of me as my jinrikisha was whirling past the positively irresistible sign,

SAVINGS & CUTINGS OF HAIRS WITHIN.

THE LANGUAGE

Would that I had let the wheels still whirl! For one's experience outside the "baber sop" is far funnier than when we are once in the little crazy chair before the mirror that makes one look like a composite photograph. In the first place, things are not clean; in this respect the tonsorial parlors seem to be the exception that proves the rule of Japanese cleanliness. In the second place, the barber does not understand English, which is inconvenient for strangers, since one is likely to lose a cherished moustache by requesting that it kindly be spared. But these are only minor discomforts. The brush itself is an instrument of torture, being about as soft as the end of a broom handle. The razor is made after the pattern of an antiquated jack-knife, minus the pivoted blade and good steel. Moreover, the executioner holds this tool at right angles to your skin, with consequences that may be better imagined than described. The sweep of his hand is something wonderful. And after he has swept your face with his scythe, he produces sundry other sinister-looking instruments, and proceeds to shave the inside of your nostrils and ears. Then he brushes out the débris with tiny scrub-brooms, breaks the yolk of an egg

JAPAN TO-DAY

in your hair, and humbly informs the honorable guest that the august shave is at an end. A little more and the guest would be in the same locality. The redeeming feature of the affair is in the fact that you have to pay only five *sen* for the performance. You then go home and shave yourself.

This is all the strict, sad truth.

I had already tried still another disastrous experiment in the matter of shaving. I had been in Japan but a few short days, remember; moreover, I was young, unfledged. Sir Edwin Arnold's gentle maunderings had informed me that a Japanese valet knows everything; and now I owned a real live valet, my first and last. Incidentally, he was cook and housekeeper and errand-boy and chamber-maid, and also a Methodist preacher; age, about fifty years. I thought that, added to his numerous other accomplishments, he certainly must know how to shave,—especially as he wore a thin, scraggy beard of his own, whereof he was mightily proud. I remember it was a Sunday morning. I took my dictionary-holder, brought all the way from America, and with it at the back of a chair to hold my lordly head, extemporized a tolerable imitation of a barber's

THE LANGUAGE

chair. Then I took my new native dictionary, and looked up the Japanese word for "shave." There it was: *Soru, Soru, Soru,* as I said it over and over again to myself.

Finally I called the docile Toku San in, and, assuming an attitude of command, ejaculated,—

"*Soru!*"

Toku San shook his head in dismay, and rapidly answered, "*Wakarimasen,*"—which being interpreted, means, "I humbly do not understand."

I understood enough to understand that, but I was bent upon using my valet. So I assumed a somewhat sterner aspect, accompanied my remark with a dignified stamp of the foot, and shouted in a tone which could not be ignored, the only word I knew upon the subject:

"*Soru!*"

Toku San was always extremely anxious to please,—the same who once went out to kill a whale for me. And now he was obviously discomfited. He scratched his head vociferously, sucked his breath in noisily between his teeth, and said,—

"*Danna San, sukoshi mo wakarimasen,*"

JAPAN TO-DAY

—" Mr. Master, I humbly do not understand a little bit."

Still one more effort I made with my sole but steadfast word, accompanying it this time, however, with a sweeping tonsorial gesture across my callow countenance. This time, Toku San evidently understood. A tremulous, but joyous, smile flitted across his utterly toothless mouth. With glad and hasty step he retired into the adjoining apartment to make the grave and necessary preparations.

Meanwhile, I became lost in the labyrinths of my darling dictionary, and did not look up for some minutes. When I did, the devoted Toku San was standing before my mirror, my own particular shaving-brush in one hand, my razor wobbling wildly in the other, his crinkled brown face creamy with imported lather, about to offer the supreme sacrifice of his tenderly-nourished whiskers on the altar of filial devotion!

After this linguistic confession of my own, I am sufficiently malicious to append one or two more kinetoscopic sketches of the wrestlings of the native mind with the complexities of English construction. The first

THE LANGUAGE

consists in a letter from a pupil who was "perfecting" his English.

"DEAR SIR: I am very glad to hear that you and your family are very well and I am also quite well as usual, but my grandfather's disease is very severe without changing as customary. I fear that it is a long time since I have pay a visit you. I wish your pardon to get away my remote crime. We have only a few hot in Saga as well as summer is over, and we feel to be very cool in morning and evening. Sometimes we have an earthquake here at now, but the mens was afright no more. I grieves that a terrible accident took place in the school of military Saga. The story of it, a scholar had put to death some colleague with a greate stick on the floor and a doctor of anatomy dissected immediately with dead disciple, then all pupils of school were now to question its matter in the judgement seat; but do not it decide yet. Unequivocal matter would speak you of kind letter."

Professor Chamberlain, in his delightful little encyclopædia, entitled "Things Japanese," cites an almost incredible quotation from a book published in Japan in 1886 for the purpose of teaching "the practical use of English conversation for police authorities." The police having to deal very largely with organs of the human anatomy, the work opens with a vocabulary of useful anatomical terms. Among these are listed "a gung," "a jow," "the mustacheo;" diseases such as "a caucer," "blind," "a ginddiness," "the megrūn," "a throat wen," and other words useful to policemen. The instructor devotes the remainder of his manual to "Misseranious Subjects," comprising typical conversations which are to be committed to memory somewhat after the order of Mark Twain's memorable Ollendorff system. Here is a supposititious dialogue between a Japanese policeman and a British blue-jacket, as recorded in this "royal road to language learning:"

Policeman. "What countryman are you?"

Sailor. "I am a sailor belonged to the 'Golden Eagle,' the English man-of-war."

P. "Why do you strike this Jinrikisha-man?"

S. "He told me impolitely."

P. "What does he told you impolitely?"

S. "He insulted me saying loudly 'the Sailor, the Sailor,' when I am passing here."

P. "Do you striking this man for that?"

S. "Yes."

THE LANGUAGE

P. "But do not strike him for it is forbided."

S. "I strike him no more."

A momentary gleam of diffidence seems to cross the police mind when one policeman says to another, "You speak the English very well," and the other replies, "You jest."

One more instance, and I am done. I cite it not only as a specimen of the woes of ambitious Japanese youth in learning English, but also because it reveals rather frankly the motive of their ambition, a motive perfectly intelligible to those who by residence among them have become acquainted with their almost frenzied patriotism, or "Jingoism," which they boastfully term *"Yamato-damashii,"* or, "the Japanese soul." I had told the advanced class in English essay to write on "Why I Study English." The conclusion of one of the brightest lads appeared as follows:

"The English is the language of the most strongest nations. Whosoever wish to conquer any country, he must know the country and get the people's confidence. But this will not be done without he understand the language. Now we will learn the English. And then our navy shall sail across the sea,

JAPAN TO-DAY

we will conquer the England, we will conquer also our dear Teacher's country, and the flag of Great Japan will wave above the all world."

Think what a catastrophe will befall the human race when "the all world" will be compelled to learn the awful Japanese language!

VI
SERMONS GARNISHED WITH SMILES

¶ The Buddhist at Church—A Sermon on the Chief End of Man—Tales from Japanese Folk-Lore—A Specimen of Oriental Humor—Religions Old and New

VI

SERMONS GARNISHED WITH SMILES

THE sensational preacher in America could well take points from the Buddhist preacher in Japan. If the aim of a model homily is to present a modicum of morals with a plenitude of diversion, then the Buddhist priest is certainly a model preacher. He is charming as a raconteur, and his "application" is never stiff enough to hurt. He is in earnest, but in earnest to amuse.

Mr. Mitford, in his "Tales of Old Japan," has in the most life-like manner sketched the preacher at his work.

"We were shown into an apartment adjoining a small chapel," says Mr. Mitford, "a room opening on to a tastily arranged garden, wealthy in stone lanterns and dwarfed trees. In the portion of the room reserved for the priest stood a high table, covered with a cloth of white and scarlet silk, richly embroidered with flowers and arabesques; upon this stood a bell, a tray containing the rolls of the sacred books, and a

JAPAN TO-DAY

small incense-burner of ancient Chinese porcelain. Before the table was a hanging drum, and behind it was one of those high, back-breaking arm-chairs which adorn every Buddhist temple. In one corner of the space destined for the accommodation of the faithful was a low writing-desk, at which sat, or rather squatted, a lay clerk, armed with a huge pair of horn spectacles, through which he glared, goblin-like, at the people, as they came to have their names and the amount of their offerings to the temple registered. These latter must have been small things, for the congregation seemed poor enough. It was principally composed of old women, nuns with bald shiny pates and grotesque faces, a few petty tradesmen, and half-a-dozen chubby children, perfect little models of decorum and devoutness. One lady there was, indeed, who seemed a little better to do in the world than the rest; she was nicely dressed, and attended by a female servant. She came in with a certain little consequential rustle, and displayed some coquetry and a very pretty bare foot as she took her place, and, pulling out a dandy little pipe and tobacco-pouch, began to smoke. Fire-boxes and spittoons, I should mention, were freely

Buddhist Priests

BUDDHIST SERMONS

handed about; so that half an hour which passed before the sermon began was agreeably spent. In the meanwhile, mass was being celebrated in the main hall of the temple, and the monotonous nasal drone of the plain chant was faintly heard in the distance.

"So soon as this was over, the lay clerk sat down by the hanging drum, and, to its accompaniment, began intoning the prayer, '*Na Mu Miyō Hō Ren Go Kiyō,*' the congregation fervently joining in unison with him. These words, repeated over and over again, are the distinctive prayer of the Buddhist sect of Nichiren, to which the temple Chō-ō-ji is dedicated. They are approximations to Sanscrit sounds, and have no meaning in Japanese, nor do the worshippers in using them know their precise value.

"Soon the preacher, gorgeous in red and white robes, made his appearance, following an acolyte, who carried the sacred book, called *Hokké* (upon which the sect of Nichiren is founded), on a tray covered with scarlet and gold brocade. Having bowed to the sacred picture which hung over the *tokonoma,*—that portion of the Japanese room which is raised a few inches above the rest of the floor, and which is regarded as the place of honor,—his reverence took his seat at the table and adjusted his robes; then, tying up the muscles of his face into a knot, expressive of utter abstraction, he struck the bell upon the table thrice, burnt a little incense, and read a passage from the sacred book, which he reverently lifted to his head. The congregation joined in chorus, devout, but unintelligent; for the Word written in ancient Chinese is as obscure to the ordinary Japanese worshipper as are the Latin liturgies to a high-capped Norman peasant-woman.

"While his flock wrapped up copper cash in paper, and threw them before the table as offerings, the priest next recited a passage alone, and the lay clerk irreverently entered into a loud dispute with one of the congregation, touching some payment or other. The preliminary ceremonies ended, a small shaven-pated boy brought in a cup of tea, thrice afterwards to be replenished, for his reverence's refreshment; and he, having untied his face, gave a broad grin, cleared his throat, swallowed his tea, and beamed down upon us, as jolly, rosy a priest as ever donned stole or scarf. His discourse, which was delivered in the most familiar and easy manner, was an extempore dissertation on certain

BUDDHIST SERMONS

passages from the sacred books. Whenever he paused or made a point, the congregation broke in with a cry of '*Nammiyō!*' a corruption of the first three words of the prayer cited above, to which they always contrived to give an expression or intonation in harmony with the preacher's meaning."

Among my chief desires on taking up the study of the language was a wish to find what manner of sermons the Buddhist priests preach to their people. Without further ado I append a translation, made in those early days, of a typical Japanese sermon. It might be fitly entitled,—

WHY DO WE LIVE?

"In a certain place there was once an extraordinary dunce by the name of Chōkichi," begins the preacher. "Now, there are very many dunces in this world, but this particular fellow was a most accomplished dunce. In the matter of forgetting things he was a perfect genius.

"One day his mistress said to him:

"'Chōkichi, this is the anniversary of the death of our principal ancestor, and his reverence the priest will be here before long. Therefore we must have the customary offerings ready to set before the household gods. So hurry to the market and buy me some carrots, dock, wild potatoes, mushrooms, and lotus root,—these five things.'

"With this she gave him five farthings, and Chōkichi, with an exclamation of assent, girded up his loins and started off.

"As he was hurrying along to market on a dog-trot, he met his neighbor Chōmatsu.

"'Hello, Chōkichi!' said the latter; 'you are in a great hurry. What are you after and where are you going, anyhow?'

"'To market to buy some things.' answered Chōkichi, as he hurried on.

"'Well, what are you going to buy?'

"'What am I going to buy? I don't know, I'm sure,' was the reply.

"So the story goes. This forgetting the important business that his mistress had sent him on, and only racing in the street—it was a great piece of folly, was it not?

"And yet, this Chōkichi is not to be heedlessly laughed at. For while it may not be true of this audience, yet in certain distant parts of the country there are many people who forget the essential thing, just as

BUDDHIST SERMONS

Chōkichi did; whereas, so far as other matters are concerned, they know everything about them. If you don't believe it, ask anybody.

"Here, Hachibei! [The preacher addresses an imaginary character.] They tell us that everything born into this world has a commission from heaven. For example, take the cow and the horse,—what were they born for? And Hachibei will answer, 'Why, anybody knows that! They were born to carry heavy loads and to save folks labor.' But the cock, what was he born for? Ask him that, and he will tell you, 'He was born to tell the hours.' The dog, what was he born for? 'He is to guard the gate.' But the cat, what is she for? 'She is to catch rats.' Ask anything you please, so far as general matters are concerned, and he knows all about them. Well, then, Hachibei, you yourself, what were *you* born into this world for? But Hachibei will scratch his head, and finally answer, 'What was I born for? *I* don't know. Most likely I came just to eat rice and find fault.' For us to think that man alone came into this world to wander purposeless,—that is for us to belong to the foolish fellowship of Chōkichi. . . . It

JAPAN TO-DAY

is man alone that has *not* come into this world just to eat rice and to grow old. Man is called the lord of the universe; of all things he is chief. He is not like the dog or the cat. It is not for him to wander aimlessly.

"But let us go on with our story. Chōkichi reached the market-place at last, but he had quite forgotten what he came to buy. And so, as he was loafing around the place with the money in his hand, he caught sight of some cakes in a shop-window. Forthwith he bought and ate about a dozen of them. Then he loitered here and loitered there; he drank a little wine and loafed in the grog-shop. He spent every one of his five farthings buying things in the street and eating them on the spot. And then he went home grumbling to himself:

"'It wasn't enough! Mistress didn't give me coppers enough! And so I can't get any fried eels or duck-hash!'

"Now, when he got home, maybe his master and mistress weren't waiting for him! And maybe they weren't hot!

"'Look here, Chōkichi, what have you been doing? Have you brought what you were sent for?'

BUDDHIST SERMONS

"When they said this, Chōkichi answered, in a dazed sort of way:

"'No, I haven't brought anything at all.'

"'But what have you done with the money we gave you?'

"'Oh, the money!' said he; 'why, I spent it all for things to eat in the street; only it wasn't nearly enough.'

"Master and mistress sat completely dumb. At length they broke out:

"'Why, what are you thinking about? The five farthings,—don't you understand? We didn't tell you to spend them in any such way as that! You were to buy carrots and dock and the rest! But instead of buying what we need, you spend them in stuffing yourself, and then on top of that you tell us that you haven't enough! You must be a perfect fool!'

"And they stormed and scolded away.

"Now, dunces are beyond redemption.

"'Why!' said Chōkichi, with a look of utter amazement, 'do you want some carrots and some dock? If that is what you want, I've just been to the market, and why didn't you tell me so? That would have been the very time to get them.'

"Well! well! He was an accomplished

JAPAN TO-DAY

dunce! And in the wide world one could hardly find a master that would keep such a fellow for five minutes. So in the end there was nothing to do but send him away with two or three cuffs across the head. However, it is quite useless for any of you to hear a story of this kind and merely roar over it. This is nothing less than a parable. And with the words of Confucius on our lips, 'If I see folly I look within myself,' to-day both you and I should well consider whether we too do not belong to the company of this Chōkichi.

"In the first place, we received at birth from our Master Heaven these admirable bodies that we call the five members. We were provided with what we call the five senses, far more precious than the five farthings,—the five functions of seeing, hearing, smelling, tasting, and feeling. In our hearts, likewise, we received at birth the five virtues of love, justice, courtesy, wisdom, and truth. And the real meaning is simply this: Heaven desires to have us buy what we call the five relations,—the carrots and the dock, which are these five things: obedience to parents, loyalty to masters, concord between husband and wife, harmony among

BUDDHIST SERMONS

brothers, and a mutual fidelity in our intercourse with others. And yet, quite forgetting the essential business of the five rules or doctrines, day and night we spend our time in nothing but this buying and eating things in the street, with its 'I want this—I want that—that will not do—or, there is not enough of this!' Why, is not this Chōkichi? It was not to wander about thus purposeless that we were born."

As the Buddhist priest goes from home to home in the administration of his duties, or as the people drop in to hear him preach, he will color up ancient stories in such fashion as that they eventually become the very folk-lore of the people—the mental pabulum upon which children are fed and youths grow into manhood. Two of these stories that I have never seen in print fell into my hands when the students were requested to write English essays on "Tales from Japanese Folk-Lore." The most of these tales were worn and wearisome, but two have a freshness and piquancy that entitle them to a place in this chapter; for they are nothing else than "sermons garnished with smiles," as the reader may discover for himself. To me they have added zest because of the quaint English phrasing of the really talented young essayists. The first might be fitly entitled,—

THE TRAPPER TRAPPED; OR, THE WAY OF
THE TRANSGRESSOR IS HARD.

"In olden times there lived a farmer who had three daughters, in a little village. He possessed a few acres of rice-field which he cultivated diligently. In summer, when the rice plants began to bloom, the bright weather continued too long. Ditches and streams were dried, and of course the rice plants were on the point of being parched with drought. The poor farmer, earnestly desiring to revive them, tried to supply with water, but all in vain.

"One day, he at last advertised that to whomever could fill the field up with water he would give his daughter as reward. Next morning he visited the field expecting to find the plants dying. But what was his gladness when he came to it! The plants were very green with dew, instead of yellow. The field was full of water, instead of being dried. He said to himself: 'I wonder who was able

BUDDHIST SERMONS

to do this? It would be beyond the capacity of human beings. Who was he? How fortunate I was to have the plants brought out of withering!' After walking around the field with great joy, he returned home.

"About half an hour after, a peculiar voice was heard at the door. The delighted farmer, suspecting, went to the door, and when he opened it, he found a wild, hairy monkey standing there, to his surprise. The visitor said, 'Last night I filled your field with water, working very hard. So I have come to receive such a reward as you said in the advertisement. Please give me your daughter.' He turned pale when he thought of putting one of his favorite daughters in the hands of such an ugly beast. He greatly regretted that he had acted so rashly. But whoever the claimant might be, he never could refuse what he had promised. He resolved to give, and called to his presence the eldest, and told her to become the wife of the monkey. Another trouble happened. She denied her father's request. 'I should rather,' said she, 'die than become a beast's wife,' and ran away. Then he called forth the second, and tried to persuade her, in vain. But the youngest was very obedient to parents, and easily assented to her father. 'It is an easy matter,' said she; 'please give me a mirror and a jar. I like to have such things.' The father soon gave them, partly with easiness, and partly with the sorrow of parting. The jar fastened to the monkey's back by encircling him with a cord, and the mirror held in the girl's hand, the strange couple hastened to the forest.

"Oh, what an unhappy creature! Was she to live her unpleasant life in a dark cave or on a high tree, one time met by a wolf, and the other by a large serpent, instead of having visits from her dear friends from her old agreeable home? No; heaven would never desert so obedient a daughter. About a mile's walking brought them to a bridge across a deep river. While looking on the river, the poor girl dropped her mirror into the water on purpose, but as if by mistake. She showed a sign of great alarm, and cried out: 'Oh, I have lost in the water my favorite mirror! Nobody will help me! I should prefer to drown to living without a mirror.' Pretending to weep, she lay down on the ground. 'No,' said the monkey, fearing to lose his lover, 'no; you need not cry for it. I shall be able to find the mirror out

BUDDHIST SERMONS

and to place it in your hands. Wait a little.' In an instant, he jumped into the water, nay, into Hades, because the water poured into the jar on his back, and he was drowned after struggling with the waves for a minute. The young widow walked home in triumph, and spent her happy days with her father and sisters."

I shall not moralize on the content of these ethical discourses. The reader who is so disposed may do that for himself; for they are in truth extremely suggestive indexes to the ethical ideals of a race. The selection that follows will show that sometimes a heathen may even quote Scripture to suit his purposes. I shall accordingly entitle it,—

CAN THE BLIND LEAD THE BLIND?

"Once upon a time there were two men, one of them named Hachibei, and the other Gonsuke. They were very strange.

"Once these two men were travelling from Kyōto to Yedo. Then when they reached the river Tenryū, it seemed that the bridge had been washed away by the heavy storm of the day before. So passengers that came to this river were tucking up their trousers to cross the river.

"When Hachibei and Gonsuke were intending to do so, two blind men came, and one of them, named Ittukū, asked them whether it was possible to cross the river. Hankū, the other of the blind men, asked, 'Is the water as high as your knees?' Hachibei replied, 'Yes.' Then Ittukū said to Hankū, 'As you are younger than I, please carry me across.' 'Foolish fellow,' said the other, 'what a cheeky fellow you are!'

"At last they drew lots, and the old Ittukū won. Then Hankū was obliged to carry the other. 'Now, are you ready? Come on! Come on!' So saying, he got ready, and turned his back to Ittukū.

"But Hachibei seized this opportunity, and jumped on his back. Hankū, the young blind man, thinking him to be his friend Ittukū, immediately entered into the river, and carried Hachibei to the other side.

"'Oi! Oi!' said the old blind man, who was remaining on the other side; 'what are you doing?' Hankū, on the other bank, hearing his voice, said with anger: 'What a cheeky fellow you are! I have just carried you across, so why did you go back again?'

BUDDHIST SERMONS

"Ittukū said, 'You must not speak like that to your elder; come quickly and carry me over.'

"At last Hankū was obliged to cross back again. 'Now,' said Hankū, offering his back, 'you may jump on.' But Gonsuke, without hesitation, put out his arms and jumped on his back. As Hankū entered the river again, Ittukū, in breathless excitement, called out, 'Where are you?'

"Hankū, who was now in the middle of the stream, exclaimed, 'Oh, this sly fellow! Who is this?' and let Gonsuke fall into the river with a splash.

"'Help me! help me!' cried Gonsuke. Hachibei then jumped in and pulled him out of the water. And he was wet through. '*A-a-a-ah-kuso!*' said Gonsuke; 'that blind rascal has done me a shabby trick.' '*Wa! Ha! Ha!*' laughed Hachibei.

"At this Gonsuke said, 'As you set the example, I fell into the water. How cold it is!'

"So saying, he proceeded to wring out his clothes. Then the blind men came across the river. At last Gonsuke got a cold.

"'Do men gather grapes of thorns, or figs of thistles? Even so every good tree bringeth forth good fruit; but a corrupt tree bringeth forth evil fruit. Every tree that bringeth not forth good fruit is hewn down, and cast into the fire.'"

These "sermons garnished with smiles" must inevitably produce the impression that the Japanese are frivolous. This impression is essentially correct. That is to say, they are the gayest and most irrepressibly mirthful folk in all the world. They live on the crust of molten volcanic fires, they tremble almost daily with the terrible chill of the earthquake, and they are used to the thunderous blast of the tempest,—but in it all they are the same cheerful, happy-hearted, and pleasure-loving people. They will treat a funeral as though it were a feast, and even their sermons are garnished with smiles. But the broadest of these homiletic smiles I have kept for the last. It is told in one of their most familiar books of moral lectures, and the reader may discern its "moral" for himself. Possibly it will not have great zest for those who are unfamiliar with Japanese ways and customs. But to me, "sermon" though it be, it is far and away the finest

Around the Brazier

BUDDHIST SERMONS

specimen of quaint Oriental humor that ever came under my ken. Perhaps it might be called,—

CIRCUMSTANCES ALTER CASES; OR, THE FOLLY OF THE APE.

Once upon a time,—so runs the story, which I quote from memory,—a certain bald retainer called upon his lord and master, to have a long talk about various matters pertaining to the management of the large estate. It was winter, and when the noble lord came in, he saw to it that a liberal supply of glowing charcoal embers sent forth their grateful heat from a brazier set between them on the floor. Thus they sat flat upon the mats and talked, the retainer now and then uttering exclamations of astonishment at the wisdom of his sage employer, who was known far and wide for his sound sense and unfailing presence of mind. The while they talked, this latter quality received fresh and convincing illustration. For the charcoal, snappy and saucy in the frosty air, suddenly sent a glowing ember leaping into the very lap of the stately lord, full upon his handsome apron of brocaded silk. The bald retainer flew all to pieces in his helpless anxiety to relieve the situation—gazing wildly around for some implement to remove the red-hot coal, and sputtering like a sperm-whale in his excitement. But meanwhile, the master, with a calm remark to the effect that it was of no consequence whatever, had quietly inserted his hand beneath his silken apron, and, with the skilful "chuck" of a boy playing marbles, had shot the saucy fire-ball back into its proper place before it had even scorched the precious silk. When the excited retainer at length comprehended what had happened, he sat back upon his haunches speechless with admiration, unable to do anything but utter an occasional "*Naruhodo!*" of rapt amazement over such marvellous presence of mind. He had learned a lesson,—ever hereafter would he strive to emulate the matchless wisdom of his lord. Meanwhile, the lord sat talking as though nothing had happened, to his faithful, if somewhat abstracted, servitor, whose thoughts were now fixed on loftier themes than tenantry and rents. Would that he might have opportunity to imitate the wisdom of his master! As luck would have it, the opportunity was not long delayed. For the malicious charcoal once more vented its

BUDDHIST SERMONS

fiery spleen, a living coal leaping this time straight for the flat bald head of the retainer, where it lay and glowed with wrath. It was now the master's turn to become excited. He looked from side to side for some implement of relief; he clapped his hands wildly to summon the maid,—and exclaimed:

"Why, man, that coal will burn straight through into your stupid brain!"

But the retainer sat perfectly cool and collected, an expression of calm and elevated superiority upon his suffering brow.

"Never mind," he murmured; "it is of no consequence whatever,"—and, mindful of his lord's example, reached up and chucked himself under the chin!

The three great pagan systems that have directed the spiritual development of the Japanese are Shintō, Buddhism, and Confucianism. The first of these, or "The Way of the Gods," is native to Japan; the other two coming from India and China, respectively. Æsthetics and filial piety are the foundation-stones of Shintō. Morality, as we understand the term, has nothing to do with Shintō as unaffected by contact with Christendom.

JAPAN TO-DAY

Native writers, indeed, have denied that the Japanese stand in need of any moral instruction. One of the greatest disciples of Shintō is on record as saying that "in Japan there is no necessity for any system of morals, as every Japanese acts aright if he only consults his own heart. Morals were invented by the Chinese because they were an immoral people." Filial piety is the great, the sole commandment of the law. It should continue even after the death of its object. Hence the origin of Shintō, which is chiefly ancestor worship. But the æsthetic tastes of the people prompt them to the poetical expression of this worship. Therefore the chosen sacred places are spots of great natural beauty,— nature building more noble monuments than man. As has been already said, every wooded dell and silvery cascade, each limpid lake and lofty hill, is consecrated by a shrine to the memory of the reverend dead. Far from morality inhering in the Japanese conception of religion, phallicism was until recently an integral part of Shintō.

Buddhism was imported by way of Korea about the middle of the sixth century of the Christian era. With their customary intellectual hospitality, the Japanese accepted it

BUDDHIST SERMONS

with open arms. And with remarkable plasticity Buddhism moulded itself towards the encompassment of Shintō, so that now the two cults are often inextricably interwoven, though the Shintō share of the woof is sometimes exceedingly small. In the seventeenth century Shintō made an effort to recover its independence; and even now, for obvious political purposes (since it teaches the divinity of royalty), it is the recognized religion of the state. But Buddhism, the gorgeous religion of India, is enormously more attractive of devotion than the childish Shintō, and wields even now a powerful sway over the ignorant masses. Its enormous educational influence in the past was pointed out in the opening chapter.

Buddhism is a singularly inconsistent system. It deifies the forces of nature into innumerable gods, but does not teach the doctrine of a personal god; it is, in fact, atheistic. It believes in the perpetuation of existence through innumerable and ever-varying forms, but teaches that our highest goal is non-existence. It derives its greatest strength from the immortal personality of its illustrious founder, Sakya Muni, but minimizes the idea of personality in ourselves. Its motto is knowledge, but its Japanese devotees are confined to the ignorant multitudes. While deifying moral ideas, its priesthood is so grossly immoral that the Japanese government found it necessary not long ago to issue an open reprimand against them. The essential content of the average Buddhist sermon is exemplified by the typical discourses already presented. And even when the priest does allow himself to dwell upon the solemn themes in which his religion abounds, he will conclude his exhortation with a ludicrous grimace, as though he regarded the whole performance as a joke. Sermons are preached in the larger city temples on an average of once in ten days, and are poorly attended when judged by our own ideas.

But the people are still very devoted in the matter of temple worship proper. And many of the worshippers are more than mere ceremonialists; they are evidently very much in earnest. "See that mother leading her toddling child to the image of Binzuru, the god of healing, and teaching it to rub the eyes and face of the god and then its own eyes and face. See that pilgrim before a bare shrine repeating in rapt devotion the

A Nagasaki Buddhist Temple

BUDDHIST SERMONS

prayer he has known from his childhood, and in virtue of which he has already received numberless blessings. Behold that leper pleading with merciful Kwannon of the Thousand Hands to heal his disease. Hear that pitiful wail of a score of fox-possessed victims for deliverance from their oppressor. Watch that tearful maiden performing the hundred circuits of the temple while she prays for a specific blessing for herself or some loved one. Observe that merchant solemnly worshipping the god of the sea, with offering of rice and wine. Count those hundreds of votive pictures, thanksgiving remembrances of the sick who have been healed, in answer, as they firmly believe, to their prayers to the god of this particular shrine." These are all actual cases. And Mr. Gulick points out, in his "Evolution of the Japanese," that they are the evidence of a profound religious instinct, which persists in spite of all the abuses of religion.

Confucianism is not a religion at all. It is a cold and heartless system of ethics. Coming to Japan at an early date from China, it long remained useless and dormant. But through the influence of the great Emperor Iyeyàsu it began to displace Buddhism as the national preceptor early in the seventeenth century, and has until very recently commanded at least the nominal allegiance of the more intelligent classes of the Japanese. But the most recent reports are to the effect that "Confucian philosophy, sociology, and statecraft have had a great fall from their former high place. Confucius is a deserted leader, inconspicuous among the many heroes whom Japan has crowned. Even Seido, the historic temple of Confucius in Tōkyō, has been appropriated for an educational museum. The old religions exercise no moral power over the student class of Japan, and religious teaching is not allowed in the curricula of the new government institutions." Japan presents the strange spectacle of a people with a deep religious instinct who are rapidly losing hold of their old religious systems and have not as yet firmly grasped the new.

But one of the most significant signs of the trend of things is in the fact that Christianity is beginning to influence and transform the pagan religions themselves. We are told on every hand that a new spirit is abroad, for example, among the Buddhistic priesthood. "Their preaching is increas-

BUDDHIST SERMONS

ingly ethical. The common people are saying that the sermons heard in certain temples are identical with those of Christians." And Buddhism is not the only imitator. Missionaries who have attended the services of the most modern forms of Shintō have been surprised to hear almost literal quotations from the Sermon on the Mount, although the speaker was unconscious of the source. Mr. Gulick adds: "It is evident that Christianity is having an influence in Japan far beyond the ranks of its professed believers. It is proving a stimulus to the older faiths, stirring them up to an earnestness in moral teaching that they never knew in the olden times. It is interesting to note that this wide-spread emphasis on ethical truth comes at a time when morality is suffering a wide collapse."

Meanwhile, the little sacred "Bible" of the Japanese people continues to be the famous "Imperial Rescript on Morals in Education," promulgated by the present ruler, Mutsuhito, in the year 1890. It is supposed to embody the quintessence of Shintō and Confucianism combined, and is the only authoritative moral teaching allowed in the government schools. "It is considered both holy and inspired." Here follows a translation of this very remarkable document, to which four and a quarter million of Japanese students listen at stated intervals with heads bowed in reverent awe,—the only authoritative moral guide recognized by Japan today:

"The Founder of Our Empire and the Ancestors of Our Imperial House placed the foundations of the country on a grand and everlasting basis, and established their authority on the principles of profound humanity and benevolence.

"That our subjects have throughout the ages deserved well of the state by their loyalty and piety, and by their harmonious co-operation, is in accordance with the essential character of our country; and on these very same principles our education has been founded.

"You, our subjects, be therefore filial to your parents; be affectionate to your brothers; be harmonious as husbands and wives, and faithful to your friends; conduct yourselves with propriety and carefulness; extend generosity and benevolence towards your neighbors; attend to your studies and practice your respective callings; cultivate

BUDDHIST SERMONS

your intellects and elevate your morals; advance public benefits and promote the social welfare; ever render strict obedience to the constitution and to all the laws of the land; display your personal courage and public spirit for the sake of the country whenever required; and thus support the Imperial prerogative, which is coëval with the Heavens and the Earth.

"Such behavior on your part will not only strengthen the character of our good and loyal subjects, but will also conduce to the maintenance of the fame of your worthy ancestors.

"This is the instruction bequeathed by our ancestors and to be followed by our subjects; for it is the truth which has guided and still guides them in their own affairs and in their dealings towards aliens.

"We trust, therefore, that we and our subjects shall regard these sacred precepts with one and the same heart in order to attain the same ends.

"Given at Our Palace in Tōkyō this 30th day of the 10th month of the 23d year of Meiji (1890)."

VII

LIFE IN THE SOUTH

¶ The Island of Kyūshū—A Calm Succeeded by a Storm—The Land of the Unknown Fire—A Sketch of Saga—Life in a Japanese School—Side-Lights on "Demoniacal Possession"

VII

LIFE IN THE SOUTH

DURING four out of the five years that I spent in the Island Empire my address was "Saga, Hizen, Kyūshū." In the original meaning of those three simple words you have a history which is also a story, and a story of the most interesting sort, telling the truth that is stranger than fiction.

Let us begin backwards, Japanese fashion, and analyze "Kyūshū" first—a name that has become somewhat familiar here, because of the excellence of Kyūshū rice. Its literal meaning is "nine provinces,"—whereby hangs a tale. Japan consists of an indefinite number of small islands (some four thousand by actual count), and the definite number of four larger ones. These four mainlands, of which Hondo is chief and central, stretch in the form of a narrow crescent, a thousand miles from north to south. The northernmost is icy Yezo, where the aboriginal Ainu lives. Shikoku lies just south of Hondo, while Kyūshū stretches still farther towards the equator, lying in the latitude of the State of South Carolina. These four mainlands were in ancient times, for purposes of government, divided into eighty-four large provinces, nine of the largest of which constituted the "nine provinces" of Kyūshū.

This large southern island has had full share in the shaping of the history of the nation. From these coasts, several centuries before the Christian era, Jimmu Tennō, the first Japanese emperor, is alleged to have set forth on his career of adventurous conquest. Hence also the great expeditions of the Japanese Amazon, Jingō Kōgō, and of the illustrious "Taikō," Hideyoshi, went forth to successful warfare in times of old against the neighboring country of Korea. It was on the soil of Kyūshū that the first European missionary landed, in the year 1549, and from that day onwards, even during that period of three hundred years of eremite seclusion that succeeded the anti-Christian revolt in 1587, Kyūshū it was, alone of all Japan, that kept in some slight touch with the Western world. Finally, the battle of Shimonoseki Straits, in 1864, confirmed Commodore Perry's opening of all

IN THE SOUTH

Japan to the comity and the commerce of the nations; and it was in the very town of Saga, in a most romantic manner to be hereinafter recorded, that the first fruits of Protestant missionary effort blossomed from the seed of God's Word.

It was on the last day of the year that I fought my own personal battle with the waves of Shimonoseki Straits, and conquered the gates of Kyūshū. Our voyage from Yokohama to Kōbe had been exceedingly stormy, our trim little Japanese steamer tossing like a man with the fever and quivering throughout her whole frame like a man in the grip of the ague. Five hundred native fishermen lost their lives off the coasts near us that night.

From Kōbe to Shimonoseki the weather was fair, and we viewed with delight the beauties of the Inland Sea. Many experienced travellers deem this the most enchanting bit of sailing in the world. The water lies placid as a pool, save only where disturbed by the turbulence of mysterious whirlpools, which will sometimes seize a great ship and spin her around like a top. Jutting from the land-locked ocean rise countless little verdant isles, carved into grotesque shapes, among which the ship picks her way with the dainty skill of a woman. Often we seem completely encircled by land, our entrance shut fast behind us, and no exit visible in front. Then, with arch sidewise motion, the vessel glides through a hitherto hidden gateway and begins once more to thread the maze of evergreen islands. Toy houses stand on the shining beachlets. Toy islanders run to and fro. Tiny sails glisten like bird-wings flitting through watery groves. Overhead, marvellous turquoise skies arch a roof for this veritable fairyland, this miraculous garden of the sea.

But when we reached Shimonoseki the storm returned with redoubled violence. There were no other passengers to disembark, and for a long time I failed in securing a boat that would land me in the storm. Finally a good-sized scow that had brought coal out to our steamer, and was lashed to her side safe and sound, undertook the task for a consideration. I clung to the single mast, with its sail reefed tight to its sides. The waves tossed us like a fleck of foam, yet I did not think we were in very great danger until within a few hundred feet of the shore. A wall of solid masonry is built

IN THE SOUTH

up there, to protect the land from the encroachments of the sea. Our fishermen crew had to beat around this wall with their sturdy oars in order to reach an inlet of safety. But just at the critical point, the sail ripped suddenly loose, the men lost control of the boat, and the furious wind dashed us with a fearful shock and crash, sheer against the frowning stone wall. Once again, and yet once more this happened, the side of our boat being shattered in splinters, and the water submerging us fast. All of this took but an instant. But at the third crash occurred a feat I have never in my life seen equalled, nor, under the circumstances, have I any strong desire to look on the like again. Just at the one possible instant, before the boat crashed the third time against the wall, a little nimble lad shot up the mast like a monkey, a long rope around his thighs, and leaped through the air to the shore! A hundred eager hands of shouting, gesticulating natives seized the shore end of the rope, pulled us instantly taut and snug, and gently hauled our battered craft around the mole to its haven. It was the one chance in a million. The next crash would certainly have crushed our foothold from under us,

JAPAN TO-DAY

and flung us to the merciless sea. A dozen fishermen and I owe our lives this day to the daring skill of a little unknown lad. It was a feat which any who have watched Japanese acrobats can believe in; but, I verily believe, possible only to these nimble, sure-eyed people.

New-Year's morning dawned bright and clear, the town alive with the festival. At dawn I made my way briskly to the train, the air being bracingly cold. All who were early astir wished me a happy new-year. An old man I had never seen before grasped my left hand with his right, thinking this the proper thing to do with a foreigner, waved my digits from left to right a few times, and wished me a most honorable congratulation. He happened to be a railway porter, so I asked him whether he couldn't bring me a tin heater for my feet, as there was nothing of the sort in the car, and all of the Japanese trains are supposed to carry them. He replied voluminously, kept the train waiting several minutes, and finally returned with a pair of tin spittoons. He had apparently imbibed rather freely of some primitive new-year's beverage.

So it was that I journeyd to Saga. A

Boy Acrobats

IN THE SOUTH

light fall of snow lay on the ribbed rice-field outside, so that they looked like great griddle-cakes with a frugal sprinkling of sugar. Snow in the province of Hizen, despite the fact that the name means "fire"-land!

But this warm name has nothing to do with the climate. The reason for this name is bound up with the strangest thing I saw in this strange land. Hizen is called "fire"-land because it borders on the sea of the "unknown fire." On a certain night in every year, at one specific hour, one may see from the summit of a sacred hill a great ball of fire rise out of the sea a few hundred yards from land, break into a million dancing sparks; then reassemble its fiery forces from the shimmering dancing-floor, and majestically fade into the night whence it came. If you get into a boat and row out into the sea, nothing is visible. Scientists, both native and foreign, have made the matter a subject for investigation, without result. The phenomenon has recurred for ages, hence the names of the two bordering provinces, Hizen and Higo—the "nearer" and the "farther" provinces of the "unknown fire." Mine own eyes have seen it, the while my skin was creeping.

JAPAN TO-DAY

Having dissected the words "Kyūshū" and "Hizen," finally we come to Saga itself.

More than four hundred years ago, while Japan was steeped in the petty wars of feudalism, there grew in a wide and fertile plain a number of gigantic, flourishing trees. Their wealth of growth and beauty was so great that the people round about called them *Sakura,* a word formerly used to denote prosperity. The transition is easy. When, finally, a prosperous city had encircled the stately trees, its busy citzens found *Saga* easier to say than *Sakura,* and said it,—just as our lazy English speech has slipped eventually all the way from *episcopos* to "bishop."

To write the history of Kyūshū would almost fill a library, that of Hizen would more than make a book, and I may hope to give only the briefest sketch of Saga in this short chapter. But, such as it is, I write it on account of its interest as a picture of feudal Japan.

As the young historian would say, go back with me four centuries, and find a country governed by a nominal Mikado and powerful clans of warriors, the latter constantly at war among themselves. One of the hardier

IN THE SOUTH

leaders, Suseyoshi by name, built for himself a great castle at the beginning of the sixteenth century, and he built it where the lordly trees were growing. The growth of his house was as that of the trees, so that, in 1562, his grandson Takanobu united various small dominions under one government, and caused this capital of Saga to become a very rich and busy place, deserving of its name. The castle was extended; gigantic walls of huge stone masonry were built around it, many of them remaining to this day. Humble hovels were converted into magnificent mansions, and small shops became big bazaars. Strengthened in his power and glory, Takanobu went forth again to war, and conquered the neighboring provinces of Chikuzen, Chikugo, and Bungo, with half of Higo. The greater part of Kyūshū would doubtless have come under his sway had he not fallen in the bloody battle of Shimabara, in the year 1584.

He was succeeded by his son Masaie, who inherited the warlike spirit of his father. But a greater than he was in the field, for the celebrated general, Hideyoshi, the persecutor of the Christians, eventually drove all foes before him, Masaie along with the rest.

JAPAN TO-DAY

Yet Hideyoshi was generous enough to give the government of a considerable territory into the hands of his conquered enemy, who, however, feeling that he had enough of war, soon retired from active life, giving his power in turn over to his boyish son, who had been entrusted to the guardianship of a worthy farmer's son named Nabeshima. This rustic guardian was wise and brave and ambitious. It was not long until his usurpation of power had so enraged the rightful ruler that the young prince, passionate but helpless, took his own life. Thereupon Nabeshima's son was appointed legal successor, and the prosperous rule of the Nabeshima family began, only to terminate in the great revolution of 1868, when the prince of Saga returned all his lands to the restored Mikado. The present Nabeshima is a marquis, with a handsome home near Saga, which he sometimes visits, though his head-quarters are in Tōkyō. I taught school daily in the ancient castle, which has lost its former splendor, though it is not by any means devoid of interest even in its ruin. Here and there in the city grow stately camphor-trees, finer than any others in all Japan, fully justifying the origin of the name of Saga. While

IN THE SOUTH

the city has declined from the high position of wealth to which it once attained, it is still prosperous, with its rice exchange, its great stores, its government of a large section of Kyūshū under the crown, and its excellent schools.

Saga has given its name to one of the numerous petty wars that followed the restoration of 1868. It was in 1874 that an adventurous spirit named Eto returned to this city from his position under the government in Tōkyō, and attempted to incite rebellion—if such it may be called—in order to undertake an expedition for the subjugation of Korea. Japan has always been uneasy about Korea. But he and his followers were conquered, so that all that remains besides their memory are a few bullet-holes in the castle wall. Yet their memory is certainly kept fresh. Within a short distance of the old feudal "palace" which became my home, stands a monument in memory of these defeated soldiers, of striking design and most noteworthy workmanship. It consists in a huge tapering, cylindrical pedestal, built of heavy masonry, surmounted by a turtle,—the Oriental emblem of eternity,— upon whose back stands a tall, unpolished

JAPAN TO-DAY

stone, which bears the simple memorial inscription. People come here to admire and to worship, although their loyal allegiance is freely given to the national government now, just as many of us in the South are true Americans, while devoted to the memory of Lee. Not far from this Eto monument is a large temple, built and dedicated in honor of the soldiers that fell in devotion to their leader.

I came to this old-fashioned town to teach these Japanese Southerners the language of the Anglo-Saxon peoples, for ambitious purposes which some of them, as we have seen, were subsequently frank enough to expose. When the day of inauguration came, the principal of the school informed me that my presence was desired, in order that I might be formally introduced to the boys. This principal was a pleasant, dignified man, with a fair knowledge of English. He received me most kindly, and, after a little chat in the school parlor, the teachers were marched in and presented to their new associate. There were eighteen of us altogether. My own official position in the school was

IN THE SOUTH

next to that of the principal; who, by the way, was an officer of the government of no mean rank. Things are carried on with all due ceremony in this school, which is, of course, a government institution,—of the ordinary middle grade. The principal has his secretary, a sort of prime minister, discharging the actual duties of his superior. Then there is a treasurer, and a disciplinarian. The latter drills the boys daily in military tactics.

After this general greeting from the teachers, the principal said to me, "Now let me introduce you to my boys—*our* boys." So we proceeded to the large entry hall, where the drill-master had massed his company of three hundred and thirty sturdy fellows in a closely-packed square. A temporary stand had been erected, from which the principal made a short speech of introduction. After I had made a shorter one, the boys gave a stiff military salute, and I was from that time regularly installed as a teacher in the school.

My duties consisted in teaching Conversation and Composition, Reading, and Dictation. I would go to the school at ten in the morning, and leave at three in the afternoon. An interval of thirty minutes is allowed at noon for lunch. There is also a recess of ten minutes between classes, which are taught an hour at a time. Each class has its separate room, where the teacher goes to meet it. The teachers have a large room to themselves in the second story, each with his desk, chair, and small brazier containing charcoal. The only stove in the building is in the centre of the teachers' room, and as it is impolite to wear an overcoat in the presence of company, the sole resource for the shivering foreigner is to wear his overcoat under his undercoat, so to speak. I kept myself comfortable by enveloping in heavy flannels, three vests, and a heavy short coat. But I often felt ashamed when I saw those boys sitting there in their thin *kimonos,* with their throats exposed, and their brown legs bare. The teachers say it is a part of the boys' education to teach them to endure. They are surely patient, manly, polite, and studious fellows, though some of them are insufferably conceited.

The building in which our school was long conducted is an ancient castle, to which allusion has already been made. It is enclosed by a massive and very old stone wall, about

IN THE SOUTH

which is a deep, wide moat, in which grows every year a crop of beautiful lotus flowers. The castle is a rambling, two-storied building, quite unlike the European castle. Many of its windows are of paper, affording but little protection from the wintry blasts. The roof is of tiles, the timbers very heavy, the ceiling low, arched, and dusky with paint and years. At the gate in the heavy wall is a porter's lodge, from which a clear-voiced bugle sounds out the daily calls to duty. Near by this lodge is a weather observatory, with its anemometer and its time-gun, which latter is fired every day at noon. A full retinue of servants is employed in and about the building, ready at all times to do the teacher's bidding.

The branches taught are English, German, Chinese, Japanese, General History, Geography, Mathematics,—embracing Algebra and Geometry; Chemistry, Physics, Ethics, Zoölogy, Drawing, Agriculture, Gymnastics, and Military Tactics. The course requires five years, the boys coming to this school from a primary school, and going hence to a still higher academy, whence they are sent to the Tōkyō University for a finish. Saga happens to be an

JAPAN TO-DAY

educational centre, for it contains, besides the large institution in which I taught, a primary school, a large normal school, and several schools for girls. One can hardly turn a corner without meeting some student, in his funny costume, consisting in a flowing robe, bare legs, wooden shoes, and a German blue-cloth cap, on the front of which is a Chinese character showing to what school he belongs. Our students all have their rooms apart from the castle, coming there only for recitations and public exercises. The chief of these public exercises consists in a unanimous worshipful bow before the picture of the Emperor. Patriotism is strongly inculcated; it would be difficult to find anywhere a set of people more in love with their country than are the Japanese students.

Especial attention is paid to the study of English. Out of the eighteen teachers, no less than six of them instructed in that foreign tongue, while only one taught German. Besides the branches under my direction, Grammar, Spelling, and Translation were taught by the native teachers.

By and by the government built us a brand new school building, and moved us out of

Southern School-girls

IN THE SOUTH

the castle. One fateful night a drunken teacher of morals upset his ash-tray on the matting, and the new building was soon aflame from end to end. In the midst of the fire I witnessed a striking illustration of the intensity of Japanese schoolboy patriotism. I came upon a group of seniors, woe-begone and actually weeping. When they saw me, one of them sobbed,—

"Oh, teacher, we are filled with the sorrowful!"

I tried to console him with the assurance that we should have a new building finer than the one now burning.

"No, no!" he said; "it is not the building that sorrows us; our Emperor's picture is burn!"

It was a photograph that could be replaced for less than a dollar; but the fact that the Emperor was being treated with disrespect by having his picture burnt meant more to these frenzied young patriots than the destruction of their fine new school. I am very sure that any one of them would cheerfully have risked his life to rescue the cremated photograph.

Classes of students and teachers flocked to my house each week to study the English

JAPAN TO-DAY

Bible. It was the language alone that they cared for; but now and then the power of the living Word would win them almost in spite of themselves, and lead them to love the Gospel.

I think it is worth while to mention here one of the interesting experiences that occurred during our study of the life of Christ. When the teachers' classes came to the first mention of the subject of demoniacal possession, I expected them to raise grave objections, and had endeavored to prepare for persuasion. For these teachers are bold and alert in their use of the methods of rationalism, and are usually incredulous to the core. To my surprise, however, they treated "possession" as a matter of course. It is a common belief in Japan, where the "demon" is always embodied in a fox. For the benefit of such as are interested in this subject, I append the following remarks of an eminent German rationalist employed in the Imperial University at Tōkyō, who has had peculiar opportunities for the study of these cases in a large hospital under his charge. For this I must again acknowledge indebtedness to Professor Chamberlain.

"Possession by foxes (*kitsune-tsuki*) is a

IN THE SOUTH

form of nervous disorder or delusion, not uncommonly observed in Japan. Having entered a human being, sometimes through the breast, more often through the space between the fingernails and the flesh, the fox lives a life of his own, apart from the proper self of the person who is harboring him. There thus results a sort of double entity or double consciousness. The person possessed hears and understands everything that the fox inside says or thinks, and the two often engage in a loud and violent dispute, the fox speaking in a voice altogether different from that which is natural to the individual. The only difference between the cases of possession mentioned in the Bible and those observed in Japan is that here it is almost exclusively women that are attacked—mostly women of the lower classes. Among the predisposing conditions may be mentioned a weak intellect, a superstitious turn of mind, and such debilitating diseases as, for instance, typhoid fever. Possession never occurs except in such subjects as have heard of it already, and believe in the reality of its existence.

"The explanation of the disorder is not so far to seek as might be supposed. Pos-

JAPAN TO-DAY

session is evidently related to hysteria and to the hypnotic phenomena which physiologists have recently studied with so much care, the cause of all alike being the fact that, whereas in healthy persons one-half of the brain alone is actively engaged,—in right-handed persons the left half of the brain, and in left-handed persons the right,—leaving the other half to contribute only in a general manner to the function of thought; nervous excitement arouses this other half, and the two—one the organ of the usual self, the other the organ of the new pathologically affected self—are set over against each other. The rationale of possession is an auto-suggestion, an idea arising either with apparent spontaneity or else from the subject-matter of it being talked about by others in the patient's presence, and then overmastering her weak mind exactly as happens in hypnosis. In the same manner, the *idea* of the possibility of cure will often actually effect the cure. The cure-worker must be a person of strong mind and power of will, and must enjoy the patient's full confidence. For this reason the priests of the Nichiren sect, which is the most superstitious and bigoted of Japanese Buddhist

IN THE SOUTH

sects, are the most successful expellers of foxes. Occasionally fits and screams accompany the exit of the fox. In all cases—even when the fox leaves quietly—great prostration remains for a day or two, and sometimes the patient is unconscious of what has happened.

"To mention but one among several cases, I was once called in to a girl with typhoid fever. She recovered; but during her convalescence, she heard the women around her talk of another woman who had a fox, and who would doubtless do her best to pass it on to some one else, in order to be rid of it. At that moment the girl experienced an extraordinary sensation. The fox had taken possession of her. All her efforts to get rid of him were vain. 'He is coming! he is coming!' she would cry, as a fit of the fox drew near. 'Oh! what shall I do? Here he is!' And then, in a strange, dry, cracked voice, the fox would speak, and mock his unfortunate hostess. Thus matters continued for three weeks, till a priest of the Nichiren sect was sent for. The priest upbraided the fox sternly. The fox (always, of course, speaking through the girl's mouth) argued on the other side. At last he said: 'I am tired of her. I ask no better than to leave her. What will you give me for doing so?' The priest asked what he would take. The fox replied, naming certain cakes and other things, which, said he, must be placed before the altar of such and such a temple, at 4 P.M. on such and such a day. The girl was conscious of the words her lips were made to frame, but was powerless to say anything in her own person. When the day and hour arrived, the offerings bargained for were taken by her relations to the place indicated, and the fox quitted the girl at that very hour.

"A curious scene of a somewhat similar nature may occasionally be witnessed at Minobu, the romantically situated chief temple of the Nichiren sect, some three days' journey from Tōkyō into the interior. There the people sit praying for hours before the gigantic statues of the ferocious-looking gods called Ni-ō, which are fabled to have been carried thither from Kamakura in a single night, on the back of the hero Asaina, some six hundred years ago. The devotees sway their bodies backward and forward, and ceaselessly repeat the same invocation, *'Na Mu Miyō Hō Ren Go Kiyō! Na Mu*

IN THE SOUTH

Miyō Hō Ren Go Kiyō!' At last, to some of the more nervous among them, wearied and excited as they are, the statues' eyes seem suddenly to start into life, and they themselves rise wildly, feeling a snake, or maybe a tiger, inside their body, this unclean animal being regarded as the physical incarnation of their sins. Then, with a cry, the snake or serpent goes out of them, and they themselves are left fainting on the ground."

Time fails me to tell more of these four strange years, spent in a Japanese school. I should, however, be unjust to myself and untrue to my alien associates if I failed to mention their conduct in a time of serious trial. For the day came when the insidious climate wrought its work on overstrained nerves, and the plans of my life were changed by the imperative orders of physicians. What I wish to say is, that in those days of mist and fog, when I stood a helpless stranger in a strange land, knowing not whither to turn or how,—no friends could have been gentler, more considerate, more helpful than those dusky pagan Southerners, under whose silken vests beat the hearts of as chivalrous gentlemen as ever brake lance in a tourney. Saladin was a pagan. And when I think of those Japanese gentlemen and their gentle deeds in the days when they were true "friends in need," I feel like erasing from these pages every sentence which is not a compliment, every criticism that is not a tribute; while their beautiful word of parting has for me an added new meaning: *Sayōnara—If it must be so!*

VIII
THE PEOPLE OF THE NORTH

⁋ The Aborigines of Japan—
Ainu Characteristics — King
Penri—Strenuous Pastimes—
The Spiritual Traditions of a
Primitive People

VIII

THE PEOPLE OF THE NORTH

IT is a far cry from Saga to Sapporo. When a man breaks down from "Japanese head," or brain exhaustion, in the peculiarly oppressive climate of Southern Japan, the first expedient is always a trip to the bracing climate of the North. Yezo is an island almost as different from Hondo and Kyūshū as though it belonged to another continent. And I shall never forget the keen delight of the bracing Northern air that summer when I had to lay down my work ingloriously and go questing for fresh gray matter. I may say here, however, that while Yezo helped, it did not heal; therefore, after several months of vain experiment, the doctors drove me all the way across the ocean, and told me to stay at home.

Sapporo is a town that lies in the heart of Ainu land. The Ainu are the aborigines of Japan, so far as we can know. There are traces of a still older race, but it is not improbable that they were simply the ancestors

JAPAN TO-DAY

of the present Ainu. This much is clear: that when the Japanese conquered their island empire it was by driving the swarms of Ainu slowly northward until at last the vanishing remnant lodged in the farthest North, precisely as with a similar case in England. Localities in every section of Japan still bear Ainu names; in fact, it is not unlikely that Mount Fuji itself was named by the Ainu in days when its fires were still active, as "the goddess of fire," though this is a question of dispute.

It would be hard to find two peoples more thoroughly unlike than the Ainu and their Japanese conquerors. I am free to confess that, in some respects at least, the difference seems to me to be in favor of the Ainu. They are lazy and dirty to a degree; but there is an openness and honesty about them that one looks for in vain among the possessors of "that restless Japanese eye" of which Dr. Griffis speaks. To me, there was the same tonic relief in passing from the one people to the other as was brought by the change of climate. Among the Japanese, no matter how friendly they might be and often are, one always feels that he is living among aliens; with the Ainu, he somehow

THE AINU

knows that he is with friends. There are many indications of their Aryan descent, and consequent kinship with us. They are certainly of a totally different race from their conquerors.

In physical appearance the Ainu are much more prepossessing than their neighbors— taller, broader, straighter, more sturdy altogether, and with luxuriant patriarchal beards that make the possibly envious Japanese deride them as "hairy dogs." The more aged men inspire a positive feeling of veneration. As they would come to the doors of their huts, during the tour I made with their beloved missionary chieftain through the very thick of their conquered land,—as they would stand with stately gesture and musical benediction of "Peace," one was inevitably reminded of the Biblical pictures of Abraham and Moses and the prophets, and half tempted to think that these modern Oriental patriarchs had just stepped from the vistas of antiquity.

I am well aware that other travellers have scorned "the hairy Aino" (as the name is improperly spelled), and have seen nothing but their dirt and shiftlessness. Every one must speak for himself, however, and I for one cannot withhold admiration from a race at once so crushed by their conquerors and yet with their "milk of human kindness" quite unsoured,—a race gentle and confiding towards strangers, because they trust one another, as the Japanese seldom or never do, —a people as brave in the chase as though each one were a Nimrod, and who therefore cannot be justly called cowards,—a people who, although they have no arts and no letters, are saturated through and through with an abiding sense of the spiritual.

I was more fortunate than other travellers have been in the manner of my introduction. There is but one European who thoroughly understands the Ainu race, and that is my noble friend the Rev. John Batchelor, who for many years has toiled with ceaseless consecration in their service. He has reduced their language to a written form and grammar, and collected various specimens of their remarkable mythology and folk-lore. To his learning and kind helpfulness this chapter owes whatever value it may hold.

Allow me to introduce the reader to a real king: Penri, king of the Ainu. For the munificent sum of five cents, this royal, Lear-like personage not only condescended to be

THE AINU

sketched in all the splendor of his regal garb, but also presented me, into the bargain, with a handsome willow *inao,* or votive offering, which still adorns my walls. Penri lives in the Ainu capital of Piratori, a squalid village of some hundred and fifty souls, all kin. He has in his time been a doughty man of the chase—bear-killing having been his favorite pursuit. On one of his feet you may see a token of his cool pluck and presence of mind in danger. Quite unlike the other islands of Japan, Yezo abounds in poisonous serpents, the most deadly being the viper. Penri received in the forest one day a fang-stroke full upon one of his toes, and with as little concern as though removing a splinter, sat down and amputated the stricken member *instanter.*

His curse has been the curse of all the Ainu, the sin of drunkenness. The wretched wine-vendor of the conquering race has proceeded against these simple huntsmen with the same weapon that unscrupulous Americans used against the Indian, with the result that the Ainu, like our own aborigines, are a rapidly vanishing race. Formerly inhabiting the whole of Japan, their number is now reduced to a paltry fifteen thousand among

JAPAN TO-DAY

the mountains of Yezo, and, unless signs fail, a few years more will witness their entire extinction.

Despite their servile subjection to their conquerors, the Ainu still show in the chase a hardihood and primitive bravery that could scarcely be surpassed. Where can one find a more spirited description of adventure than Mr. Batchelor's account of an Ainu bear-hunt?

"In very early spring, when the snow is quite hard, so that a person can easily walk upon it, the Ainu take their dogs and go to see if they can find a bear's den. The dens are recognized by a slight discoloration of the surface of the snow, in the centre of which a small hole is to be seen. This is caused by the warm breath of the animal inside. If successful, prayers are said, the snow is cleared away, and long sticks poked into the den to try and drive the bear out; the dogs, too, are set to worry the beast. Sometimes the bear comes out and is shot, but at others it refuses to stir.

"If neither sticks nor worrying dogs can stir the beast, a fire is lighted over the mouth of the cave, and smoke is tried. This is said to be generally successful, but not always.

THE AINU

"Some bear-hunters say that bruin absolutely refuses to kill anything in its own den. Therefore, if a bear will not come out when requested, in the ways above mentioned, a brave Ainu ties his head and face up, leaving only his eyes exposed; hands his bow and arrows to his friends, and, with his hunting-knife firmly fixed in his girdle, makes a call upon the bear in its home. The animal gets so angry and surprised at this that it unceremoniously seizes the intruder with its paws, and hastily thrusts him behind its back. The Ainu now draws his knife and pricks the beast behind, and this is said to make it take its departure. Of course, as soon as the animal gets outside, a few poisoned arrows are sent into its body.

"This is the critical and dangerous moment; for the bear, now in pain and full of wrath, furiously attacks its enemies. If it comes to very close quarters with a man, and stands upon its haunches ready to strike him, this is considered to be a golden opportunity; for the man throws aside his bow and arrows, and, drawing his knife, rushes into the animal's embrace and thrusts the knife home into its heart. This kills the beast in a moment. But the man who does this hardly ever gets off free; he is pretty sure to get scratched, sometimes very severely, and some, we are told, have been nearly scalped and killed in this way."

Even their favorite games are of sufficiently strenuous character to satisfy the most exacting. "Ukara" is nothing more nor less than the whipping-post used as a pastime. The contestants, one after another, bare their backs and grasp a stake or tree. Then a practised executioner seizes a long wooden club with but a thin sheathing of cloth on its business end and proceeds to lay on blows that are apparently as hard as he can possibly bestow. The winner is the man who is last to cry, "Enough." If any foreign spectator expresses doubt as to the actual energy of the blows, administered with such apparent severity, the executioner will smilingly offer to let the skeptic see for himself.

We were in the heart of Penri's country at the time of a total eclipse of the sun, scheduled to be visible in Yezo more favorably than in any other quarter of the globe. Only a few miles from us an elaborate temporary observatory had been established by enthusiastic American astronomers who had

THE AINU

crossed the Pacific for no other purpose than to be present in Yezo for the one priceless hour of a century. But, alas! when the eventful hour arrived, the heavens were obscured by a pall of impenetrable cloud, and we were afterwards told that certain members of the astronomical party were completely prostrated with disappointment.

As for us, we also missed a coveted opportunity—the sight of an Ainu community in the dreaded presence of a solar eclipse. Their traditions as to this phenomenon all run somewhat as follows:

"When my father was a child he heard his old grandfather say that *his* grandfather saw a total eclipse of the sun. The earth became quite dark, and shadows could not be seen; the birds went to roost, and the dogs began to howl. The black, dead sun shot out tongues of fire and lightning from its sides, and the stars shone brightly. Then the sun began to return to life, and the faces of the people wore an aspect of death; and as the sun gradually came to life, then men began to live again."

Mr. Batchelor tells us that the sun is supposed to be the residence of a goddess, who is its ruler and life and light. If the goddess disappear from her dwelling, the blackness of course ensues. The people are therefore greatly terrified by an eclipse, and cry out, "The sun is fainting away! the luminary is suddenly dying!" Not only so, but they endeavor to revive the goddess, by flinging water upwards into her fainting face, with the incantatory prayer, "O goddess, we revive thee! O goddess, we revive thee!" An eclipse is the more serious to their imagination, inasmuch as, despite their ignorance, they have subtle enough knowledge of nature to believe that heat is almost synonymous with life; their best way of bidding a person farewell consisting in the fervent words, "May you be kept warm!" The dying away of the sun would therefore mean to them, as to us, the dying away of all life.

This is but one example of the remarkable spiritual intuitions of this simple yet subtle-minded race. A still more striking illustration is in their belief that the earth is round. Apparently they evolved this faith from their own inner consciousness, as the ancient Chinese and Japanese, in common with the whole world before Columbus, believed the earth to be flat. Yet the Ainu teach that "the world is a vast round ocean, in the midst

THE AINU

of which are very many islands, or worlds, or countries." Their word for the various divisions of land is always "floating-earth," preceded by some qualifying adjective to denote the size or location. If asked why they believe that the world is round, they give the remarkable answer: "Because the sun rises in the east, sets in the west, and comes up the next morning in the east again."

These wonderful folk believe that evil came into the world by means of a "tree of evil," while their ideas of the chaos that existed when the earth was as yet "without form, and void," sound almost like a paraphrase of the opening words of Genesis: "In the beginning the world was a great slushy quagmire. The waters were hopelessly mixed up with the earth, and nothing was to be seen but a mighty ocean of bare miry swamp. All the land was mixed up, aimlessly floating about in the endless seas. All around was death and stillness. Nothing existed in this chaotic mass; nothing moved, for it was altogether incapable of sustaining life; nor were there any living fowls flying in the airy expanse above. All was cold, solitary, and desolate. However, the clouds had their thunder demons, and the Creator lived in the highest heavens with the hosts of subordinate deities. Then the great God determined to make the earth inhabitable."

Enough has been written to show that the Ainu entertain very remarkable religious ideas. Perhaps the most interesting feature of their faith consists in the fact that while they are polytheists, like the Japanese, with an indefinite number of tutelar deities, they yet recognize as superior to all these minor gods one supreme God "towering above all, who is the Maker of all the others, and to whom all are responsible, for they are His servants and deputies." Him they call, "God the Maker of places and worlds, and possessor of Heaven;" while their single word for "God" conveys the beautiful significance, "The Over-Shadower," or "He who covers." Sometimes also they call Him, "the Support," "the Pillar," "the Upholder;" while another beautiful name is, "The Cradle." "Just as a child is nursed in the bosom of a cradle, and is made comfortable, and kept free from danger in it, so all men are brought up and nursed, as it were, in the bosom of God; for He is the Creator, Support, Sustainer of the universe, and the Protector of all mankind."

THE AINU

"Ainu babies are left in their cradles quite alone for hours, while their mothers have gone far away to work in the gardens, or to bring in firewood from the mountains. Of course the little ones cry lustily for their mothers sometimes, but they soon learn the virtue of quiet patience, and to know that, after all, they are not forsaken, but are in a safe and secure place. So, say they, human beings should exercise the like patience, knowing that whatever happens they are not forsaken by God, and are secure in His keeping."

Mrs. Isabella Bird Bishop, who spent a few weeks in Yezo, says, in her "Unbeaten Tracks in Japan," that "it is nonsense to write of the religious ideas of a people who have none, and of beliefs among a people who are merely adult children. The traveller who formulates an Aino creed must evolve it from his inner consciousness." Mr. Batchelor, who has spent more years among the Ainu than this excellent lady spent in weeks, says of them truthfully that "they are an exceedingly religious race. They see the hand of God in everything. The world, indeed, is His temple, Nature His book, every man His priest." He says that he has never yet met the Ainu who does not, before drinking wine, return thanks for divine benefits. A common form of "grace" is, "O God, our Nourisher, I thank Thee for this food; bless it to the service of my body."

It is remarkable, however, that the Ainu will not allow their women to pray, and for reasons that are somwhat amusing. An old Ainu has explained it thus: "The women as well as the men used to be allowed to worship the gods and take part in all religious exercises; but our wise and honored ancestors forbade them to do so, because it was thought they might use their prayers against the men, and more particularly against their husbands. We therefore think with our ancestors that it is wiser to keep them from praying."

Woman is held by the Ainu (or "Man") in great contempt, though he has a wholesome fear of her anger. A legend frequently used as a lecture against female chattering thus accounts for the rugged west coast of Yezo:

"It is said that this island of Yezo was made by two gods, a male and a female, who were the deputies of the Creator. The

Ainu Man and Wife

THE AINU

female god had the west coast allotted to her as her portion of work, and the male god had the south and eastern parts assigned to him. As the goddess was proceeding with her work, she happened to meet with the sister of Aioina Kamui, and, instead of attending to her duties, stopped in her work to have a chat with her, as is the general custom of women. Whilst they were talking, the male god worked away and nearly finished his portion of labor. Upon seeing this, the female god became very much frightened, and, in order not to be behind time, did her work hurriedly and in a slovenly manner. Hence it is that the west coast of Yezo is so rugged and dangerous. If, therefore, any one is disposed to grumble at the very rough and dangerous condition of the west coast of Yezo, he should remember that it is not the Creator Himself who is at fault in this matter, but His deputy. The chattering propensity of the goddess was the original cause."

Perhaps the resentment of the Ainu towards their chattering goddess has been somewhat lessened, here of late, since it is reported that the hostile movements of the Russian vessels are impeded by the very rough and dangerous condition of the west coast of Yezo.

For the admonition of disobedient children there is a legend which accounts for "the man in the moon" as follows: "In ancient times there was a lad who would neither obey his father nor his mother, and who even disliked to fetch water; so the gods, being angry, put him in the side of the moon, as a warning to all people. For this reason, let all the world understand that the words of parents, whether they be good or evil, must be obeyed."

The cosmology of the Ainu clearly recognizes the principle of dualism. There are the gods of the sea, for example. "Their names are Shi Acha (the rough uncle), and Mo Acha (the uncle of peace), and they are brothers. Shi Acha, who is the elder, is ever restless, and is continually pursuing and persecuting his brother. He is the originator of all storms and bad weather, and is the direct cause of all shipwrecks and deaths from drowning in the sea. He is much feared, but never worshipped. Mo Acha is the god of fine weather. He it is who is worshipped at all the seaside fishing-stations, and it is to him that the clusters of *inao* one

THE AINU

may often see upon the seashore are generally offered."

Perhaps there has never been a race with a firmer belief in immortality than the Ainu. This is with them so strong that they have never used the "death penalty" as a mode of punishment, for in their eyes that would be no penalty at all—it would simply remove the criminal into a sphere where his identity would be continued and intensified, but without any pain or sorrow. This sense of spiritual survival is the most marked feature of the Ainu creed. It extends to every existing object. The spirit or essence of that which has once existed will endure throughout eternity,—whether man, or animal, or tree, or piece of furniture. With them the term "inanimate" is therefore meaningless, as all objects will be animate forever, and preserve the same identity. This faith, it will be noted, is entirely different from the doctrine of transmigration or metempsychosis, which implies a change of being or of form. The Japanese, apparently, have but a vague sense of personality. The Ainu, on the other hand, regard identity as such a profound and unalterable truth that they will never wittingly bestow the same name upon

JAPAN TO-DAY

two different persons. "Should such a thing be done, it would be looked upon as a kind of theft, and treated accordingly." The name pertains to the individual; the individual exists forever; therefore his name is his alone by sacred and inalienable right.

Their language and many of their customs are pervaded with this abiding presence of the spiritual and eternal. Their great mountains and rivers and winds are "the mountains of God," "the rivers and winds of God," and an especially beautiful flower is known as "a flower of God." Life is "a shining like the sun," and death is known, not as death, but as "a riding into the setting sun," or as "a having space for thought." Our prosaic "Milky Way" becomes with them the especial "River of the Gods," whereon the gods at play go angling for the silvery star-fish. Wherever among the mountains they find some secluded spot all tapestried with vernal beauty and canopied with the gloom of lofty trees, there they pass in reverential silence, as in the presence of divinity. My friend relates that one day, when coming down a river in a canoe with two Ainu, they chanced to pass some very bold cliffs that ran sheer down into the

THE AINU

water. There were several openings in these rocks that led into deep and thickly wooded dells. The tops of the cliffs were well wooded, and at the base of them the water was dark, slow, and deep, with a series of eddies gently rippling. Altogether the place was exceedingly beautiful, quiet, and awe-inspiring. On nearing this place the men ceased rowing, took off their head-dresses, became quite silent, and only moved enough to steer their little craft. On asking why they did this, my friend was immediately requested to remain silent for a short time, because God had His home in that place, and it behooves all men to keep silence in the presence of the Deity. So these brave and gentle folk, crushed and oppressed and ignorant, are yet strong in the hope of the eternities, and wise with that knowledge which teaches them to endure as seeing Him that is invisible. Whom they have ignorantly worshipped, is now being clearly made known unto them; and they are learning that best of all truths about God,—" God is love."

IX

JAPANESE TRAITS

¶ Topsy-Turvydom—Negative Traits: The Contempt for Time, the Absence of Nerves, Want of Sympathy, and Lack of Confidence—Positive Traits: Frugality, Politeness, and Industry—The Japanese and Chinese contrasted

IX

JAPANESE TRAITS

THE fact that God "hath determined the bounds of our habitation" gets new meaning when one has travelled and observed in the Far East. Geographical barriers may, indeed, be easily surmounted, as when the steamship skims across the great gulf that divides America from Asia. But there are other bounds, other limits, that are impassable. The first time I ever saw this truth expressed was in the writings of that brilliant French traveller, Pierre Loti, when he says that no matter how intimately the Occidental and Oriental races intermingle, there will always subsist a subtle, elusive, but real and radical difference, that will make it quite impossible for one ever thoroughly to comprehend the other.

One is not long in the East before he perceives that this is true. He sees at once that he is in a different world, where every aspect of the life about him startles with its complete novelty and surprise. Even the

JAPAN TO-DAY

face of nature wears different lineaments from those to which we are accustomed. The foliage—the whole flora, in fact—is different from ours. Physicists say that the elements of the Japanese atmosphere are mingled in peculiar proportions. The predominant curves of the mountains are convex instead of concave. There are strange fish in the sea, strange birds in the air, strange creeping things upon the ground. And if one sends a telegram home to-day, it is likely to get here yesterday!

But the people are strangest of all. They are our veritable antipodes. So opposite are their customs to our own, that one is half inclined to think himself dreaming, like Alice in Wonderland, where everything was upside down and topsy-turvy. Professor Chamberlain has dubbed Japan with the nickname, "Topsy-Turvydom." You take up a book, and find that it begins where ours end, the word "finis" coming where we put the title-page, while the foot-notes are printed at the top, the lines running downwards instead of crosswise, and from right to left instead of from left to right. You go to a dinner: it is served on the floor, and the first course is dessert. You

Carpenters at Work

JAPANESE TRAITS

go for a ride, and find that the horse will let you mount only from the right-hand side, and that he will insist on standing backwards in his stall, with his head thrust out through the door, and his tail where his head ought to be. Boats are hauled on the beach stern first. The sailors will not say, "northeast, southwest," but "eastnorth, westsouth." Nurses carry children not in their arms, but upon their backs. Carpenters pull their planes and saws, instead of pushing them; yet when they use that awkward tool the adze, comically true to the principle of contrariety, they cut from themselves instead of towards themselves. The first time I saw a carpenter using an adze, I had to laugh. But when I told him why, it was his turn to laugh.

"Why," said he, "how perfectly absurd! To chop towards yourself would be to cut yourself!"

And I saw that it all depends upon the point of view.

Building a house, these funny carpenters construct the roof first; then, having numbered the pieces, they break it up again, and keep it until the substructure is finished. When the house is done, you will find that the keys turn in instead of out. And when guests come to see you, politeness prompts them to remove not their hats, but their shoes. Finally, the color of mourning is not black, but white; and the Japanese, true to life even in death, has himself buried in a sitting posture.

These may seem to be mere superficial differences, but they really indicate a profound mental divergence between the peoples of the East and West. We think in different terms, along different lines, and reason on different principles to different conclusions. No American can ever thoroughly understand a Japanese. He may think, after dwelling among them for a few weeks, that he knows them, but longer residence corrects this false impression, and at length he is likely to give up the task in despair. Miss Scidmore depicts the people as " the embodiment of a bewildering variety of contradictions, the attempt of a race to enfold in its sentiments and customs the largest amount of opposing characteristics." We may quote the apt words of Dr. Ladd: " Obviously and traditionally polite to the verge of obsequiousness, they appear capable of the most extreme insolence. Flinging away life

JAPANESE TRAITS

for trifles in their readiness to display a self-sacrificing courage, they are—when judged by Anglo-Saxon standards—often guilty of the most culpable meanness and cowardice. Having the most delicate æsthetical sensitiveness in certain directions, they are in other directions surprisingly oblivious to all sense of proportion and propriety. Out of the noblest sentiments and impulses originate with them some of the most hideous of crimes."

If there is one characteristic that impressed me more than any other it is the wonderful gentleness of this race. And yet the man whose etiquette is as faultless as a June sky, whose gentleness of demeanor is positively captivating, may the next day perpetrate an atrocious cruelty. The driver who is so gentle as to say "That!" to his horse instead of something worse, will beat the poor beast till it drops in the road and dies. If the Japanese are gentle, they are also cruel: a paradox, but seemingly unquestionable.

So it is that Japan is a puzzle, and the Japanese are puzzledom personified. Nobody understands them. Observant and intelligent men that have lived there for a

JAPAN TO-DAY

score of years are most hesitant in rendering judgment as to the true national characteristics. Half of the missionaries contradict the other half. Every little coterie has its own pet theory, which the next little coterie derides. If all that has been written about Japan—from the abusive "North Star and Southern Cross" to the puerile and adulatory "Japonica"—should be collated and compared, the result would be a worse tangle of contradictions than the extant portraits of Columbus.

Therefore I venture to think that a feature of this book which critics may seize upon and cavil at is in fact not a defect at all: I mean its apparent inconsistencies. A book that tells the truth about Japan has got to paint an inconsistent portrait in order to be true to the life. The only device by which the Japanese may be called in any sense consistent is to say that they are "consistently inconsistent," as has been shrewdly said of Simon Peter. If, as Emerson somewhere declares, consistency is the bugbear of small minds, then the Japanese must by inference be the most catholic-minded people in the world. The present volume, therefore, has not been cut to fit a theory. It

JAPANESE TRAITS

purports to be a series of glimpses, caught at different times and from diverse angles, of the varied phenomena that make Japan the kaleidoscope it is. I have tried simply to lay the facts before the reader, and let him draw conclusions for himself.

This is by way of qualifying the somewhat ambitious attempt of the present chapter. Here we lay the telescope aside, and use for a little while the microscope; endeavoring to probe the inner character that makes the "traits." In this and in the final chapter I have called to my assistance, in a general sort of way, the most discerning critic that has ever written of Oriental characteristics from a Western point of view: Dr. Arthur Smith, whose mode of analysis for China can scarcely be improved for Japan. Without further ado, then, I shall plunge into the subject, because it has seemed to me that no book about Japan could possibly be complete that does not try, albeit with confessed incompetence, to lay bare the inner features that distinguish this peculiar race from the races that are kin to us, and therefore commonplace.

JAPAN TO-DAY

Let us look first at the negative traits of the people—and by this I mean the emphatic absence of certain attributes that to us seem fundamental and, indeed, inevitable in a civilized and enlightened nation. The practical negation of "morality," as we understand the word, was emphasized in an opening chapter; here we are dealing in a somewhat larger fashion, namely, with psychology rather than ethics, with mental traits rather than moral, perhaps, although the reader will see that the two fields touch at vital points, after all. But concrete illustration will serve better than abstract discussion. Take, for example, the negative attitude of the average Japanese mind towards the important question of *time*. It would appear to be an attitude of poorly disguised contempt. One would think that the importation of railways and telegraphs would have taught them that "Time is money;" but this lesson has yet to be learned by the masses. I am not speaking now of those thoroughly Westernized "Yankees of the East" that make up the Japanese navy, for example. The world has lately had witness that they have learned the full value of time. But take the untouched multitudes. No foreigner that

JAPANESE TRAITS

has lived in Japan can ever forget the terrible word, "*Tadaima.*" It means, "By-and-by;" which is to say, "Never." That is the answer which invariably meets the nervous foreigner as he seeks to know when some labor in which he is deeply interested will be completed by the native workmen.

Once we had occasion to level a piece of farming ground near the house; it was to be beaten down hard and smooth. We thought that an able-bodied man with a stout maul could do the task in a few days. It speedily appeared, however, that such was not to be. We were told that the work would not be done at all unless a dozen men were engaged, with a foreman, thirteen in all—unlucky number! Submission was made to the inevitable. When the men appeared, their entire equipment consisted in a single maul. Around the base of it were attached a dozen rings, to which a dozen small ropes were fastened. The men stood in a large circle around the maul, each man holding a rope. The foreman, steadying the handle with his hands, would give a signal, whereupon the dozen men would pull their dozen ropes. The result of this concerted action would be to lift the maul several feet from the ground.

JAPAN TO-DAY

Then, at another signal, the men would let go the ropes, and the maul would fall and pound the patient soil. It required thirteen men upwards of two weeks to beat down a space ninety feet by fifty. A large part of this time was consumed in drinking tea; for it was a stipulation of the contract that unlimited tea should be provided, with fire in a charcoal brazier wherewith to heat it. After every twenty or thirty strokes of the maul, intermission would be taken for tea. And yet even this ceremony was performed with infinite and most solemn industry. The typical Oriental is always working, yet never coming to the end of his work. He not only works from sun to sun, but, moreover, his work is never done.

Another negative characteristic of the Japanese is their apparent absence of *nerves*. This doubtless accounts to a large extent for the enormous amount of labor they are able to perform; for it is proverbial, with us, that worry kills more people than work. I have continually seen a Japanese subjected to the most exasperating annoyances, which would almost drive a Westerner mad; yet of nervousness there was never a trace. He will show the same imperturbable spirit under physical suffering. This is possibly due to the age-long influences of Buddhism. But the fact is indubitable that Orientals far excel us in stoical indifference to suffering of every sort.

The true Oriental is a man of colossal impassivity. Take him, for example, when he is sick. That is with us the time of all times when we must be left unmolested. Then, if never before, we demand freedom from disturbance. But with an Easterner, the opposite is the case. "The notification of an attack of illness is the signal for all varieties of raids upon the patient from every quarter, in numbers proportioned to the gravity of the disease." And the patient has no desire for it to be otherwise. Our "nervousness" is to the Japanese not only unaccountable, but quite unreasonable. In fact, they consider this as a very serious moral defect in the character of Anglo-Saxons.

To us, their absence of nerves may not seem to be a defect, but it most certainly is incomprehensible. In the steamship that brought us home, one of the crew was attacked with smallpox,—a scourge from which Japan and China are never free. The man was immediately isolated, and it became

JAPAN TO-DAY

necessary to call for a volunteer to nurse him. To the astonishment of the officers of the vessel, there was a mad scramble among the crew for this position; not out of sympathy for the patient, but because the position of nurse offered the opportunity of a holiday without reduction of wages. They were not nervous about the disease in the least; whereas the cabin passengers were in mortal terror of it.

The Japanese seem also to be strangely lacking in *sympathy*. This is to be expected, indeed, as an accompaniment of the absence of "nerves," for the sensitive are the most sympathetic. Count Mori, one of the greatest of Japanese educators, clearly recognized this defect. "Sympathy we must inculcate," he declared, "because it is the crowning virtue of civilization, and the indispensable basis of the democracy we hope, like other nations, to become. Without sympathy the best man is but a savage." This lack of sympathy often amounts, in fact, to positive cruelty. Especially is this seen in the manner with which defectives are treated. If a man has some conspicuous physical defect, it may be made the subject of continual and jeering remarks, among

The Blind Shampooer

JAPANESE TRAITS

the very classes who pride themselves on their politeness. There are few, if any, asylums for the blind or the insane. The blind Japanese have a tacit monopoly of the business of massage, and the doleful piping signal of the blind shampooer remains in the traveller's memory as perhaps the most characteristic of all the multifold street sounds. As for the insane, I have known them to be shut up in pens a dozen feet square and treated like wild beasts until death ended their sufferings. Terrible devastations, like the tidal wave which in 1896 swept thousands into the sea and left other thousands homeless, are treated by the average Japanese, unless directly concerned, with complete and contemptuous indifference.

Speaking of this apparent absence of sympathy, I shall never forget my first experience of a Japanese funeral, and a Christian funeral, at that. Here is a letter, written home the same day, when my mind was awhirl with vexed thoughts:

"To-day I attended a Japanese Christian funeral. The two-year-old child of one of the few believers in this big city died yesterday, and this afternoon I left my Bible-class in order to express sympathy with the bereaved family. Upon reaching the humble home, I found a large company of friends and relatives already assembled, seated on the floor in the main room, peacefully partaking of a feast. After bowing myself double several times, and speaking a few words of sympathy to the father and mother, I was set in the place of honor, and presented with some confections and 'honorable tea.' The tea, unsugared, in its dainty little cup, was drunk; the unspeakable sweetmeats, after a nibble, were wrapped in a paper and brought away with me, according to Oriental custom. The food is so delicious, and the supply so superabundant, that one is constrained to add to one's own store by toting the surplus home: that is the idea. But let me tell you about the funeral. The corpse was in a small wooden box, which was covered with a bright blue cloth bespangled with gilt leaves. The whole was placed in the raised recess built in every house as a place of honor; in front of it stood two plain bamboo vases filled with evergreen and scarlet berries. After the guests, seated flat around the sides of the room, had remained long enough to testify their interest, they all

JAPANESE TRAITS

wrapped up their food and prepared to form in procession. First, two boys lifted aloft two long, white banners, mounted on bamboo supports, and marched at the front. On one of these banners were inscribed the words of 1 Thes. iv. 17; I could not distinguish the other inscription. Next after them came a man with a red banner of the same pattern, bearing the child's name in ideographs. He was followed by two boys carrying the vases of evergreen and berries that had been in front of the place of honor; on the coffin itself, which came immediately after these boys, were placed crosses of cedar and red berries. I should not omit to say that the two white banners had crosses painted on them at the extreme top. By the side of the coffin walked the friend that had charge for the day; following him was the father, and behind were the masculine friends of the family, the women bringing up the rear. At the church, there was what might be called a service of song and prayer, though the presence of a noisy, giggling mob of curious loafers at the door made it seem awfully like burlesque. Nor was the levity confined to the onlookers. Among the nearest friends of the family there was frequent laughter, and more than once during the service words were exchanged all the way across the room. The procession itself, if you speak of solemnity, was more like a political demonstration in its appearance than a march to the grave.

"Far be it from me to write thus in a spirit of harsh criticism; I only design to show the inexplicable character of the people among whom I labor. One could not fail to be struck by what was more than absence of sorrowful emotion at this funeral; and yet this does by no means betoken absence of real grief on the part of the poor father and mother. What it does show is the contrariety of Japanese character—or shall I say customs?—to ours in the West. May it not be that the stoical Easterner conceals his emotion because he has been schooled to do so, while the European, encouraged by a knowledge of what is customary, yields to grief more demonstrative, yet perhaps not more sincere than that of his strange neighbor? Else is it that the failure on the part of the Japanese to recognize the existence of a true personality in each human being, and a consequent failure to set a high value on life—is it possible that such facts explain what to the Westerner seems an anomaly? At

JAPANESE TRAITS

any rate, we are antipodes. The servant that cries if you scold him a little, will laugh on the way to the funeral of his dearest friend. He may become fiercely angered over a trifle, and remain perfectly calm when a foreigner would be excited. If you tell him he is a fool he will desire to knock you down, but you may call him a liar with impunity. He is at once both cruel and gentle, gross and refined, stupid and keen-witted. Mr. Spencer would be tempted to call him a continuous series of contradictory sensations."

But the most serious negative characteristic of this interesting Oriental race is the absence of *mutual confidence.* It is almost to be doubted whether any Japanese ever really trusts another, in our meaning of that term. With us there is a wholesome adage which bids us believe every man to be a gentleman until he proves himself otherwise. But our Eastern neighbors appear to suspect from the beginning that no man is a thorough gentleman, and proof must be strong, indeed, to convince them of the contrary. Often, in Japan, I have seen lines of men, with faces covered, conducted from the prison to their trial. They wore a pecu-

JAPAN TO-DAY

liar uniform which betokened that they had been merely accused,—not convicted, or even tried. And yet they were imprisoned. Old Japanese law, the very opposite of ours, assumes a man to be guilty until he is proved innocent. The only mercy it shows him is to allow him to hide his face from public shame when led to and from the prison for his trial.

This mutual suspicion taints every feature of life in the East. It is, of course, a vast hindrance to commercial development, for Western business methods are based upon confidence. It is a sad proof, too, of the insincerity of the Oriental character; for men suspect others chiefly because they mistrust themselves. A foreign teacher, long resident in Japan, was once asked to name the leading characteristics of the people. His reply was, "Conceit and deceit." An eminent Japanese also used "alliteration's artful aid" against his countrymen when he charged them with wholesale "licentiousness and lying." The generalization is in each case too sweeping; and yet the absence of sincerity is unquestionably a Japanese characteristic. Accuse a man of a lie, and he smiles over the tribute to his cleverness.

JAPANESE TRAITS

As Dr. Smith points out, it is no more of an insult than it would be to say to an American, "You are an inveterate punster, and I am satisfied you have some atrocious pun in your head at this moment."

The most massive and monumental falsehood that ever fell to my portion was achieved by a grocer in Saga. By a lucky chance, as I thought, he was supplied at the time—so he said—with the "Golden Gate" brand of imported flour, very dear to the palate of the alien. To convince me that he was telling the truth, he brought forth an empty white bag, stamped in large English letters with the magical Western words. Well pleased that we should not need to send all the way to Nagasaki for flour, I ordered a bag sent home. An hour or so later, noting that the coolie who fetched it was so extraordinarily obliging as to carry his burden all the way into the pantry, instead of dropping it with a groan at the entry, my suspicions became aroused, and the more so as I observed that he carefully set it down with the label side turned towards the wall. Heaving the bag face forwards, I was confronted with the tame and tasteless trade-mark of the "Nagasaki Rolling Mills." The coolie insisted, however, that I, was most honorably mistaken. Knowing that he could not read English, and was perhaps deceived by his employer, I requested that the merchant himself come to see me. In a little while he appeared, smiling and patient, the empty "Golden Gate" bag under his arm for purposes of identification. Its label was printed in one color, and that of the domestic flour in another. And there stood the two diverse legends: "Golden Gate Flour" on the empty bag, "Nagasaki Rolling Mills" on the other bag. Yet that bronzed and brazen master of his art stood there, smiling and patient, and insisting with unruffled suavity that the two bags were one and the same. I almost fainted; and I kept the flour. Such mastery was not to be withstood.

The Japanese and Chinese languages—those sure indexes of a national character—are permeated with insincerity as a loaf with insincere leaven. The polite Oriental will allude to his wife, if driven to the shameful extremity of speaking of her at all, as his "stupid fool," while characterizing your own conjugal companion as "the Honorable Lady who dwells in the most honorable part

JAPANESE TRAITS

of the dwelling,"—whereas it is reasonably certain that he really entertains for this much complimented person the most profound, unutterable contempt.

Dr. Smith cites an extreme and laughable instance to illustrate the pervasiveness of honorific lying in the Chinese and Japanese languages. This incident is to me so positively delicious that I must be pardoned for purloining it bodily from his charming and illuminating pages. A visitor is represented as calling, clad in his best robes, and seated in the reception-room awaiting the arrival of his host. "A rat, which had been disporting itself upon the beams above, insinuating its nose into a jar of oil which was put there for safe-keeping, frightened at the sudden intrusion of the caller, ran away, and in so doing upset the oil-jar, which fell directly on the caller, striking him a severe blow, and ruining his elegant garments with the saturation of the oil. Just as the face of the guest was purple with rage at this disaster, the host entered, when the proper salutations were performed, after which the guest proceeded to explain the situation. 'As I entered your honorable apartment and seated myself under your honorable beam, I inadvertently terrified your honorable rat, which fled and upset your honorable oil-jar upon my mean and insignificant clothing, which is the reason of my contemptible appearance in your honorable presence.'"

So much to illustrate the more prominent negative traits that challenge the attention of Westerners. But it would be utterly unfair not to mention, on the other hand, the positive traits of Oriental character, by which I mean their strong accentuation of valuable habits of character that we possess in only a moderate degree. These positive characteristics, it will assuredly be noted, are of the highest ethical importance, and must of necessity play an important part in the future influence of the Far East in determining what races shall rule the world. Take, for example, the important question of *economy*. We simply do not know the meaning of the word. A Japanese can live and lay by a surplus where a Westerner would starve a dozen times over. Having occasion once to inquire as to the usual wages paid to maid-servants in the interior, I learned that it consisted in board and clothing

JAPANESE TRAITS

of the simplest and cheapest, and the munificent salary of three dollars and a half a year! Again, upon asking an intelligent laboring man the cost of supporting himself, his wife, and four children in ordinary comfort, I was informed that seven and a half cents a day would cover all expenses. As Dr. Smith has pointed out, Orientals remember to be economical even when they are most generous. For example, a frequent gift consists in a complimentary couplet written on paper, which is loosely basted—not pasted—on a silk background, in order that the recipient may first enjoy the poetry of the present, and afterwards its plain and practical prose; when, by removing the basted inscription, he finds himself the possessor of a serviceable patch of silk!

We may also emphasize the fact that *politeness* is an unknown art in the West. It is quite impossible for any Occidental, no matter how long he lives in Japan, ever to acquire that infinite finesse in etiquette which to the natives seems to come even as the air they breathe—most free and plenteous. From the cradle to the grave, there is a rule for every possible experience in life, which is as fixed and inflexible as brass. Woe to the

JAPAN TO-DAY

ignorant alien who does not understand it! An American lady, living in China, had recently been married. She did not know that in receiving the felicitations of her callers the bride ought to sit at the north end of the room. The callers, however, knew it very well; and, exactly true to the letter of politeness, if not to its spirit, the first ladies to call duly made their obeisances towards the northern end of the room, although the astounded bride was sitting at the south end. Was it *their* fault that she did not know where to sit? The demands of true politeness must be obeyed, despite the foolish ignorance of the despised barbarian.

My own most impressive lesson in the art of Oriental politeness occurred in an early pecuniary transaction. Upon asking a Japanese merchant the price of some fancy shells, he told me they were ten cents each.

"Now," I said to him, "you have just fifteen of them left, and I need them all. So what will be the price if I take the entire lot?"

After elaborate figuring on the ever present abacus, he replied that the fifteen would cost one dollar and seventy-five cents. Thinking that my friend the merchant had

JAPANESE TRAITS

made a mistake, or that his abacus was out of order, I confidently called attention to the fact that since all of the articles were being purchased, there should rather be a reduction in the price than an increase.

"Not at all," he replied, with a pitying smile. " I sell you my entire stock of shells. Then, when some other customer comes to buy, I, forsooth, am out. And that will be impolitely inconvenient to him. Hence, the extra charge is for my prevenient impoliteness!"—or words to that effect.

Another positive quality of the Oriental character is their untiring *industry*. No one can lodge at an Eastern inn without receiving the impression that the taverner and his help never go to bed. All night long the sleepless sounds of labor are rampant and furious. This habit of ceaseless occupation often extends to the very highest classes. A member of the Chinese cabinet being asked for an account of his daily routine, replied that he left home every morning at two o'clock, as he was on duty at the palace from three to six; and, being a member of the Privy Council, that he was engaged in that august assemblage from six to nine. As president of the war department, his duties kept him there from nine until eleven; while the affairs of the board of punishment engaged his attention from twelve till two. Finally, being a senior minister of the foreign office, he spent a part of every afternoon—namely, from two o'clock until six—with his colleagues there. But these were merely his regular duties. In addition to these matters of daily routine, he was frequently appointed to serve on special boards or committees, and these he arranged for as best he could. Surely, as the narrator wittily observes, if Solomon was right in his economic maxim that the hand of the diligent maketh rich, then the Chinese ought to be among the most prosperous peoples of the earth. "And so they doubtless would be, if there were with them a balance of virtues, instead of a conspicuous absence of some of those fundamental qualities which, however they may be enumerated as 'constant virtues,' are chiefly constant by their absence."

Now, in all of these matters the Chinese and the Japanese partake of common characteristics. And yet, just as they are facially alike, but racially distinct, so when one leaves

JAPANESE TRAITS

the mere characteristics of the people, and digs down to the bed-rock of character itself, there is a radical and fundamental divergence. Every one knows, for example, that the Japanese has proved himself to be one of the most progressive beings on the face of the earth, while China is conservatism personified. Moreover, even a superficial observer speedily discerns—what is undoubtedly true—that the Japanese intellect is alert and quickly perceptive; and he thinks that he perceives that the Chinaman is densely and incorrigibly stupid. A study of the histories of these two peoples will, however, reveal the undoubted fact that the Chinese have been great originators, whereas the Japanese, clever imitators as they are, have never created anything, with the possible exception of the field of the fine arts. The ancient civilization of Japan was borrowed whole from China, her modern civilization is borrowed whole from the West. True, they "adapt" things, by some trifling change, and make them peculiarly Japanese; but if they have ever created anything outright, it has not been shown. They scarcely have a literature worthy of the name, while Chinese literature has both depth and breadth. They have produced no great intellectual or moral leader of the world; whereas China has the proud distinction of claiming both Confucius and Mencius. The Japanese language must go for strength and massiveness to the Chinese,—being in itself frivolous, almost childish. Mr. Kipling, in fact, says that a Chinaman moving in a Japanese crowd is like a man moving among children; and Kipling has won the right to be deemed one of the keenest observers, with his fine photographic eye, that has ever contributed to English literature. Yet, forsooth, he likes the Japanese, just as we do, far better than the Chinese. In his naïve, suggestive way, he says of a Japanese city where many Chinese reside,—

"The town was full of children, and every one smiled except the Chinamen. I do not like Chinamen. There was something in their faces which I could not understand, though it was familiar enough. They had no kinship with the crowd, beyond that which a man has to children."

Yes, we like the children better, but we stand in awe of a man. And in a Chinese face, of all human faces, there is something suggestive of a hidden wisdom and power

JAPANESE TRAITS

which is altogether weird, and almost terrifying.

It is always unsafe to generalize, and yet I will venture to say that the chief cause of the marked distinction between the Chinese and the Japanese, notwithstanding their many points of likeness, lies in the fact that the former have a stronger ethical basis than their little neighbors, whereas, in the Japanese, the æsthetic predominates. The Japanese cares everything for beauty, the Chinaman cares very little for it. The Japanese laugh more than any other people in the world, the Chinaman scarcely ever smiles. The Japanese is quick to receive, the Chinaman is tenacious to retain. The Japanese is fickle, volatile, bright; his sombre kinsman is slow, but stable. The Japanese is shrewd, the Chinaman is deep. The keynote to the Japanese character is sentimentalism—that of the Chinese character is conservatism. The Japanese is a Frenchman, the Chinaman is an Englishman or a German. It is precisely the difference between the Gaul and the Teuton. The Gaul has his points of superiority. He is the more artistic, the more brilliant, the more polished, altogether the more attractive, let us say. But the Teu-

JAPAN TO-DAY

ton, while he is phlegmatic, and unmagnetic, nevertheless moves slowly but steadily, with dogged persistence, towards some predetermined goal; and when he arrives, let the world take heed!

What has Japan done for the world? She has astonished and delighted it, and rejoiced with keen relish in her own performances. But what has China done? China, not caring what the world thought of her at all, has possibly accomplished more than any other nation in history. I need only mention the three supreme contributions of Printing, the Mariner's Compass, and Gunpowder; inventions which have probably influenced the world's history more than all other inventions combined,—at least since the days when the wheel and the hinge were born,—and they all three came from China. True, for the last several centuries this immense empire has been living in the splendid achievements of its mighty past. But be sure the gigantic brain has not been idle, even in its dreams; and when, once more, the huge inert body awakens to action—let the world take heed!

X
AN OPENER OF GATES

⁋ The Personality of G. F. Verbeck—His Life Story the History of Modern Japan—The Need for Men to Succeed Him

X

AN OPENER OF GATES

WHEN word came in 1898 that the greatest of modern missionaries had passed away, the writer sent the following outline sketch of this great man to the New York *Independent*:

"The *Independent* does simple justice in setting the name of Guido F. Verbeck beside the names of Ulfilas, Augustine, and St. Patrick. I do not believe that a single Protestant missionary in Japan would dissent from this warm judgment.

"The writer of this article went to Japan in 1892, young and untried, as the pioneer of the American Lutheran mission. His board counselled: When in need of advice, consult men like Verbeck. I was often in need of advice; and he never failed in wise and cheerful aid, given with no slightest tinge of patronage, with no sign of condescension to a man of low estate, but rather as though he were the one that was favored. He made me feel at home by saying that he had been catechized and confirmed a Lutheran, his uncle having been one of our pastors in Holland.

"He believed that the plan of work should be to plant missionaries at intervals, near enough together that the intervening space would come up with Christian growth, and so the whole field be fruitful, rather than a single hill. For it is possible to overdo a policy of 'concentration' with missionaries, as with seeds. When I asked him what was the most important thing for our mission to do at first, he said: 'Get three men, so you can vote.' There is a deal of hard sense in that simple counsel.

"It may be worth while to record his judgment concerning the mooted question as to whether more missionaries are needed. As we walked one day by the lakeside at Hakone, he said, with emphasis: 'You may write to your people at home that, no matter how others may talk, I will undertake to name a hundred unoccupied points in Japan where missionaries could be placed to advantage.'

"The two things which most impressed me in this great man were his modesty and his wisdom; and by wisdom I mean wisdom.

VERBECK

He was a man to lean on; and he had knowledge as well as wisdom. To touch one point alone, there was no finer linguist in the Far East. Higher compliment could not be paid to his ability in Japanese than once fell to my hearing. A native teacher who heard him lecture in Saga said: 'He knows more of the language than I do.' This is significant, when we remember two things: the extreme intricacy and difficulty of Japanese, which led Xavier to call it the Devil's invention, and the chauvinistic conceit of the teacher.

"His humor was keen, sometimes to the point of cutting. After he had been in Japan some thirty years, one day he walked the platform at a country station, waiting for the train. A kilted, bare-legged student eyed him for a time, then concluded he would patronize this innocent alien and air his English. With that superb assurance which is the unfailing endowment of Japanese schoolboys, this eighteen-year-old colt swaggered near and shouted: 'When do you came to our country?' Dr. Verbeck adjusted his benevolent spectacles, and, after a calm survey, responded, in choice vernacular: 'A few years before you did, sir.' It is said that the student retired.

JAPAN TO-DAY

"I have in my hand his valuable pamphlet on the study of the language. He has been advising against the overuse, in sermons, of purely Chinese words, which are to native idioms as Johnsonese compounds to English. But a shrewd sense of humor prompts him to add:

"'To the caution of being sparing in the use of Chinese words, I would make one occasional exception. When you perceive among your audience a few regular pedants, put in, at or near the beginning of your discourse, a dozen or so of hard Chinese compounds, such as the greatest pedant among them cannot possibly make out,—it is the easiest thing to be done,—and you will probably find these very men your most attentive listeners to the end, although in the rest of your discourse there may be a minimum of Chinese. Simply showing such men at the start that you are not unacquainted with the trick they themselves continually use to mystify and astonish their hearers will usually make them docile to the end of your chapter.'

"He was a man without a country. Leaving Holland when young, he was never naturalized in America, nor yet in Japan; although the latter country gave him the unique privilege of a perpetual passport for

VERBECK

the whole Empire, which even the bitterest agitators of the 'Know-nothing' party never begrudged him.

"When all is said, his life is best summed up in the words: 'I determined not to know anything among you, save Jesus Christ, and Him crucified.' Untiring consecration to his Master's work ruled in all he did. His first pleasure was preaching, for which he had talents that would have made him notable in any land. I should say that his chief powers were the graphic vividness with which he could portray a scene, being richly gifted in voice and gesture; then the resistless logic with which he forced truth home. His sermons abounded in illustrations, and were the delight of Japanese audiences. Wherever he went, the people came in crowds to see and hear.

"Without him, Japan will not seem like itself. Because of him, Japan will grow less like itself, and more like the Kingdom of Heaven."

When I call Verbeck the greatest of modern missionaries I have especially in mind the untold results of his labors. In

JAPAN TO-DAY

learning, length of service, and devotion, he ranks with such men as Moffat and Paton, but the superlative degree is applicable in view of the influence Verbeck had in shaping New Japan, which may in turn shape Asia. Until Dr. William Elliot Griffis published his compendious volume, entitled "Verbeck of Japan," the world had little knowledge of the tremendous power wielded by this modest missionary, who frequently insisted, when asked for items for the press, that he preferred to "work in silence." Indeed, conditions in Japan were such that he could not have accomplished what he did in any other way. The Japanese are a peculiarly proud and sensitive folk, and they submitted to this man so largely only because they learned that his wise self-effacement made him willing always to let honor go to them when it was really due to him; as, for example, in the notable case of the great Japanese embassy of 1871, which first brought Japan to the focal centre of the world's attention, being in reality conceived, planned, and directed by this humble, unknown servant of Him who was pleased to be Servant of all.

Because the life of Guido Verbeck is essential to an understanding of the forces

A Scene near Nagasaki

VERBECK

that have made the new Japan,—because, in fact, to tell the fascinating story of his forty-five years of service is to tell the story of the Japan of To-Day, it is needful that a chapter be consecrated to his noble memory in this book.

The reader is already somewhat familiar with the old Southern city of Saga. A nobleman of this town was destined to interlock his life with that of a youth across the seas, through circumstances the most remarkable and romantic, and to become at last, by his patient endeavors, the first notable convert to Protestant missionary effort in Japan.

Being on military duty in the neighboring port of Nagasaki in the great year of 1854, charged to see to it that the hermit nation be still kept free from the touch of aliens, this lord from Saga was almost literally led through the tasting of "bread cast on the waters" to partake of that leaven which ever since has steadily been transforming his once secluded country into kinship with the Christian brotherhood of man. In a tour of naval vigilance about the harbor, he saw floating in the water a little book different from any he had ever seen before. Rescuing the curious volume from destruction, his curiosity became still more excited upon finding that the contents were stranger than the form, the book being, in fact, none other than a Dutch copy of the Gospels, which an interpreter laid bare to him with an effectiveness that enlisted his entire interest in the wonderful story unfolded. Learning that copies were to be had in the Chinese characters, and therefore intelligible to himself, he sent a man secretly to China to procure this proscribed, but coveted treasure, which afterwards, in his home at Saga, he studied with absorbed attention.

The Dutch alone, of all the people of Europe, were at that time permitted to trade with Japan, and they were confined to the little island of Deshima in Nagasaki harbor, under conditions at once severe and degrading. Somehow this little Dutch Testament was set adrift from Deshima like a Moses on the waters, to be lifted from its watery grave into the very bosom of power. And meanwhile a young Hollander, recovering from serious illness in America, had just at this moment vowed in gratitude to spend

VERBECK

his life in missionary service somewhere, little knowing that Murata of Saga, with his Dutch and Chinese Testaments, was waiting all unwitting for his coming.

Guido Herman Fridolin Verbeck was born in Zeist, Holland, on the twenty-third of January, 1830. He himself has sketched for us the simple picture of his home life, which glows with the rich colors of youth and love, like a canvas from the hand of Rubens:

"We lived like Jacob did, in the free Temple of Nature, enjoying the garden, the fruit, the flowers, with joy, on green benches, between green hedges. And after sunset, when the stars were sparkling, then we brothers and sisters went lovingly arm in arm and passed our time in garden, wood, or quiet arbor, enjoying each other's happiness and God's peace."

His education was thorough, especially in the European languages; and the profession for which he was designed was civil engineering. While still at home he fell under the influence of the Moravian missionary, Gützlaff, famous for learned and devoted work in China. The career of "Verbeck of Japan," indeed, should no doubt be set to the credit of that movement for missions which began in the eighteenth century with the Count von Zinzendorf, and has made the name "Moravian" almost synonymous with "missionary."

The story of his life before his life-work began need not concern us long. Coming to America in 1852 as to a land of promise for young men, he soon found himself ill at ease in the engineering profession, until, two years later, as we have seen, he obeyed the earlier and nobler promptings of his heart, and began to prepare himself for the ministry at Auburn, New York. The Dutch Reformed Church, feeling a sense of obligation to the newly-opened land which had long been bound by strong ties to Holland, decided to join hands with the Episcopal and Presbyterian Churches in attempting an entrance for Christian missions, and in 1859 the young minister found an opportunity to fulfil his vow in the acceptance of a call to become missionary to awakening Japan. With his bride he left New York in the sailing-ship "Surprise," May 7, 1859, in company with other missionaries, and after exactly six months of travel reached the port of Nagasaki on the night of November 7.

VERBECK

Let his own pen describe his first view of Sunrise-Land:

"With the first dawning of the day I cannot describe the beauty that is before me. I have never seen anything like it before in Europe or America. Suppose yourself to be on deck of a steamer within a port as smooth as a mirror, about sixteen neat vessels scattered about here and there, before you that far-famed Deshima, and around it and beyond an extensive city with many neat white-roofed and walled houses, and again all around this city lofty hills, covered with evergreen foliage of great variety, and in many places spotted by temples and houses. Let the morning sun shine on this scene, and the morning dews gradually withdraw like a curtain, and hide themselves in the more elevated ravines of the surrounding mountain, and you have a very faint picture of what I saw."

Nagasaki will be forever famous in connection with the history of the Christian religion in Japan. The first missionary, as has been shown, was the notable apostle of Roman Catholic missions, Francis Xavier, who came to Kyūshū from India in 1549. He and his followers had remarkable success. By the year 1587 several hundred thousand converts had been won by the missionaries of Portugal and Spain. But in that year persecutions began, under the famous "Napoleon of Japan," Hideyoshi of Saga, who by edict endeavored to expel the missionaries on account of alleged political intrigue. The great emperor Iyeyasu called fresh attention to the disregarded edicts of his predecessor, and, finally, in 1614 took the extreme position that all Christian teachers, both native and foreign, must be banished, all churches destroyed, and all believers forced to abjure their faith. This order was persistently and cruelly enforced, the descriptions of its enforcement being "beyond description horrible."

But the persecutions reached their acme under the next emperor, Iemitsu, who was terribly in earnest to execute his father's programme. As "The Mikado's Empire" tells us, "All the tortures that barbaric hatred or refined cruelty could invent were used to turn thousands into carcasses and ashes, yet few of the natives quailed, or renounced their faith. They calmly let the fire consume them, or walked cheerfully to the blood-pit, or were flung alive into the open grave about

VERBECK

to be filled up." This persecution, historians assure us, "has never been surpassed for cruelty and brutality on the part of the persecutors, or for courage and constancy on the part of those who suffered." Nagasaki, with the neighboring precipitous islet of Pappenburg, was the centre of this terrible strife, "if that can be called a strife in which there was but one side armed, but one side slain."

Finally, the salaried butchers washed the red stains from their weary arms, because the battle was over. But the government intended that its victory should be perpetual. To quote Dr. Griffis again,—" All over the empire, in every city, town, village, and hamlet; by the roadside, ferry, or mountain-pass, stood the public notice-boards, on which was one tablet, written with a deeper brand of guilt, with a more hideous memory of blood, with a more awful terror of torture, than when the like superscription was affixed at the top of a cross that stood between two thieves on a little hill outside Jerusalem." The name inscribed thereon, coupled with the most fearful maledictions against such as should confess it, was the name of Christ. "For centuries, the mention of that name

JAPAN TO-DAY

would bate the breath, blanch the cheek, and smite with fear as with an earthquake shock. So thoroughly was Christianity supposed to be eradicated before the end of the seventeenth century, that its existence was historical, remembered only as an awful scar on the national memory." To make the opening of this wound impossible, foreigners were forever prohibited entrance to Japan, the only exception being that small colony of Dutch traders shut up on a prison island at Nagasaki, doubtless favored because of their traditional enmity against the Portuguese and Spaniards. Japan put up her bars, closed all her gates, and for three hundred years was a hermit among the nations—the only light that came in from the outside world coming through the Nagasaki keyhole.

Then, in 1854, the same year that Murata of Saga tasted of the "bread cast on the waters," those gates of brass were broken, and the bars of iron were suddenly cut in sunder, by the entrance of Commodore Perry with his American warships into the bay of Yedo, demanding that Japan sign treaties of comity and intercourse with the other nations of mankind. When Verbeck

Two Brothers of Old Japan

VERBECK

arrived in Nagasaki, five years later, the awakening empire was like

> "An infant crying in the night,
> An infant crying for the light,"

and that light was in his hand.

The same Providence that set Murata's heart athirst for the waters of life, and Verbeck's heart hungry to quench that thirst, provided that these two men, whose bond of union was a Dutch New Testament, should meet each other as pupil and teacher before the new missionary had been long in his new home. For five years the silent student of the forbidden Word had treasured its truths in secret. Now, for several years after Verbeck's arrival, instruction from the missionary in Nagasaki is conveyed to the pupil at Saga through the mediation of Murata's younger brother. Finally, in the spring of 1866, Murata visits his unknown teacher, with the touching words:

"I have long known you in my mind, and desired to converse with you, and I am very happy that, in God's providence, I am at last permitted this privilege."

JAPAN TO-DAY

Later in the conversation he said:

"Sir, I cannot tell you my feelings when for the first time I read the account of the character and work of Jesus. I had never seen, or heard, or imagined such a person. I was filled with admiration, overwhelmed with emotion, and taken captive by the record of His nature and His life."

After a week of eager questioning and prayerful, patient answers, this man who for years had been reaching out towards God if haply he might find Him, received with his brother the sacrament of baptism, and returned to his Saga home committed to the outlawed faith, to which he gave loyal fealty until his peaceful death in 1874, at the age of sixty years.

It is almost incredible that in those days of fierce turbulence and civil strife, when Japan was in the throes of her second birth, an alien like Verbeck could so command the confidence of these people who would not trust each other, and who professed to hate the world. Yet men of the highest rank flocked to him for advice and teaching. His varied store of learning was made subject to continued draughts, but the supplies seemed ever inexhaustible. Best of all among his

VERBECK

many rich endowments was a superabundance of sound, hard sense, and of consecrated Christian judgment, which made him a sturdy and fearless adviser to whom the imperial government itself was finally glad to listen. Here in the classes for young men which he daily taught in Nagasaki sat scores of youth who were destined to direct the future course of empire. Supreme among these were Soejima, Iwakura, and Okuma, imbibing instruction that was steadily and withal most shrewdly directed towards the breaking down of anti-Christian prejudice, the aim to which the missionary absorbingly directed all his prayers and efforts. These men, by reason of the enlightenment they thus received from almost the only Western teacher in Japan, afterwards became cabinet officers and high ministers of state, through whom the masterly mind of Verbeck worked towards larger issues than have been faced by any other missionary of modern times.

His fame spread rapidly. By the year 1867 no less than four of the foremost princes of Japan were clamoring for him to come to their provinces and direct that foreign progress which they were so eager to advance among their people. But he was

JAPAN TO-DAY

reserved for still larger labors. Two years later he was called to the capital itself, and so after a decade of unmeasured usefulness in the Southern seaport, became the director of the Imperial University, and man-of-all-work to the newly-formed government in Tōkyō.

Here the multiplicity and importance of his labors almost defies belief. Thirty-six of his Nagasaki pupils followed him as the nucleus of a school, and shortly he was the teacher of a thousand eager learners, a second Abélard. Besides, he was busied with the translation of such great works as the Napoleonic Code, Blackstone's Commentaries, Humboldt's Cosmos, Bluntschli's and Wheaton's and Perry's treatises on political economy and international law—massive foundations for the building of a mighty nation. Nor was that all. Dr. Griffis, who saw him at his post in 1871, gives this graphic inner glimpse of the great missionary's crowded workshop:

"It impressed me mightily to see what a factotum Mr. Verbeck was, a servant of servants, indeed, for I could not help thinking how he imitated his Master. I saw a prime minister of the empire, heads of depart-

VERBECK

ments, and officers of various ranks, whose personal and official importance I sometimes did, and sometimes did not, realize, coming to find out from Mr. Verbeck matters of knowledge or to discuss with him points and courses of action. To-day it might be a plan of national education; to-morrow, the engagement of foreigners to important positions, or the dispatch of an envoy to Europe; the choice of the language best suitable for medical science; or how to act in matters of neutrality between France and Germany, whose war-vessels were in Japanese waters; or to learn the truth about what some foreign diplomatist had asserted; or concerning the persecutions of Christians; or some serious measure of home policy."

This was the time when Japan was making her mightiest strides. The changes that took place during the decade preceding 1870 seem now almost miraculous—embracing the bulk of that progress which we are accustomed, in thought, to spread over the last half-century. It is therefore interesting to find Dr. Verbeck, so long ago as April, 1870, describing the changes of "the past ten years." After pointing out that "the Japanese, ten years ago, were in nearly all respects in the same primitive condition so quaintly described in the musty pages of old Kaempfer," he says that "now the open ports and their vicinity teem with shops retailing foreign merchandise; and foreign cloths, blankets (worn as shawls), flannels, calicos, hats, boots and shoes, watches, umbrellas, and fancy articles are worn and used, in some form or other, by all classes, from the daimio to the poor 'betto' or groom. Besides the stores kept by foreigners, there are at Yokohama and Yedo alone many hundreds of native shops selling foreign goods. A large portion of the middle and upper classes—at least the male portion—dress entirely in our style. Even old men, too old to sport the new costume, look with delight upon their little grandsons dressed in hats, boots, and what belongs between, and take pride to show off in the streets their 'young Japan' thus apparelled. The army and navy are remodelled on European and American systems in organization, arms, and uniforms, down to the common trumpet, drum, and fife. We have several lines of stages, hackney-coaches, and two steamers running between Yedo and Yokohama, natives and foreigners competing with each

VERBECK

other on both elements. On the same route there is a telegraph in operation, and a contract is said to have been made for the construction of a railroad from here to Osaka. There are two extensive foundries with foreign machinery in the country, and several docks. There is a wide-spread demand, an actual thirst in many, for Western learning and science. Here is our college with its hundreds of English, French, and German scholars; besides this there are several private schools, carried on by natives, for the study of chiefly English; and there are numbers of students who study independent of any school whatever, by books and their own efforts only. Then there are hundreds more at the other open ports. There are three large hospitals and medical colleges, in which eight foreign physicians are engaged. Western medical science has nearly quite superseded the old Chinese system of quacks and immense doses of drugs. Newspapers are published in several places, with their columns of 'Foreign' and 'Telegrams,' clipped and translated from our standard home papers. Book-stores selling English and French books are seen in many places, and the quantity of books imported is prodigious."

The inhibition against Christianity, however, was still maintained in the laws, and every effort of the missionary empire-builder was aimed at this as at a target. In the summer of 1869 he submitted to the powerful Count Okuma, his former pupil, a plan that eventually accomplished the tolerance of the Christian religion, and at the same time brought Japan to a position in the front of the world-stage from which she has never since receded. This was the Great Embassy of 1871, organized according to Verbeck's suggestion, following the route he outlined, submitting to his judgment in the matter of appointments—exciting the amazed attention of the whole world, in short, while the man behind the scenes writes: "I shall leave the honor of initiating this embassy to themselves. The name is nothing, the real results are all. Who cares for the mere name and honor, if we are sure to reap the benefits,—toleration and its immense consequences,—partly now, but surely after the return of this embassy?"

Verbeck reasoned that if the leaders of the nation could but be induced to go abroad and

VERBECK

see for themselves the condition of Christian countries, they would no longer proscribe a religion that had wrought so wondrously for others. This was the motive that inspired in his masterly mind that wonderful embassy to Christendom; nor was he disappointed in his object. In fact, no sooner had the imperial ministers telegraphed from abroad their impressions, than the anti-Christian edicts disappeared as if by magic, and from that day to this religious toleration has been a principle of action in Japan!

But we must hurry on. In the year 1873, Dr. Verbeck was actually made special adviser to the Imperial Japanese Senate. Upon retirement from this important position after five years of brilliant service, he received from the Emperor the great decoration of the Order of the Rising Sun. In 1891 this "man without a country" was placed under the especial protection of the ægis of the Japanese Empire, an honor "absolutely unique" in the history of Japan. And when, on March 10, 1898, he quietly fell asleep in Jesus, the Emperor himself paid tribute to his obsequies, while military honors were observed above his grave, and an entire nation felt the touch of bereavement.

JAPAN TO-DAY

Such is the power of a hidden human life, working at one with the Master.

This sketch has but barely suggested the greatness of his missionary labors as such. Besides meeting with phenomenal success as a preacher, his share in the translation of the Scriptures is in itself a monument to make any man great forever. And not the least item to his credit is the fact that amid the turmoil of theological unrest, when the young Church of New Japan was beset with varied heresies, Verbeck stood like a rock for the old truth, which he believed to be as eternal as its source. A modest, kindly gentleman, and yet filled with all fine fearless manhood; mighty in learning, but as humble as a little child; wielding the sceptre of an empire from within the shadow of a self-imposed, modest retirement; this master of men was the servant of all, and therefore his crown is immortal. Nor shall we ever despair of the future of a race, who, for all their faults, proved so responsive to the spiritual magnetism of a holy life as did the Japanese to this master missionary.

"The openers of gates,"—the men are Christ's messengers, and the keys are the keys of the Kingdom. The key that unlocked the proud empire of Rome, and the barbarous homes of our own ancestors in Europe, is indeed a master-key, fitted to all the door-ways of the world. It is mighty in the hand of Verbeck, as it was mighty in the hands of St. Paul. Verbeck's hand has been lifted by his Master's, who called him to "Come up higher." But surely others like him must spring to take his place, that the little "gate of Asia" be opened wide to the light, so that the kingdoms of this world may indeed become the kingdoms of our God and of His Christ. "I will give unto thee the keys of the Kingdom of Heaven,"— against which not even the gates of hell can prevail. The keys of God unlock all stubborn doors, and the entrance of His Word giveth light.

XI

THE GATES OF ASIA; OR, THE LARGER MEANING OF THE WAR

¶ Palestine and Japan: "The Circuit of the Heavens"—The Vast Importance of Asia and the Present Problem of China —Russia versus Japan: The Political Argument for Missions —Reasons why Japan may Win this War

XI

THE GATES OF ASIA; OR, THE LARGER MEANING OF THE WAR

NESTLING against either side of the great mother continent of Asia are two baby countries. They are directly opposite each other, lying between the thirtieth and fortieth parallels of latitude. The shore of each is bathed by the waters of a great and famous sea: the one by the Mediterranean, which stretches out through the straits of Gibraltar into the Atlantic; the other by the Yellow Sea, whose waters mingle with the waters of the Pacific. They are similar in geography, in climate, in topography, and in many of the customs of their people. Yet, while these two countries are the twin children of the same titanic mother, they are separated not only by the imperial breadth of her capacious bosom, but also by the passage of twenty centuries. And yet, again, it would almost seem that at the close of these twenty centuries, the blessing which came out of Asia on the one side is to return into Asia

JAPAN TO-DAY

on the other side, having meanwhile belted the globe.

These countries are Japan and Palestine. It is they which lie respectively on the west and east sides of Asia, separated by five thousand miles of land and by twenty centuries of time. It is they which form the gates of Asia—Palestine opening outward, twenty centuries ago, to let the light shine out, and Japan opening inward, to-day, to let this same light, which has meanwhile traversed the intervening world, shine in.

I said, to let the light shine out. We have all heard the ancient Latin proverb, "Out of the East cometh light." It is true not merely of physical light, but of spiritual light as well. Was not the very birth of civilization with the Babylonians and Egyptians? The Great Pyramid, already two thousand years old when Abraham visited the Pharaoh, remains a fit symbol of that sublime foundation, laid first on the banks of the Nile and the Euphrates, whereon all superstructures in the arts and letters have been reared. What the lands of the Pyramid began, the eastern land of the Parthenon completed. The Parthenon to this day remains the most perfect work of art that has

Gates of the Palace at Tōkyō

GATES OF ASIA

been produced. Our highest art is but a feeble imitation of the art of Phidias and Zeuxis. And as with art, so it was with philosophic thought. The world's great trinity of intellectual giants lived in Greece, consecutively. Their influence on human life and character is still inestimable. It were not indeed too much to say that the human mind, working upward, reached its summit in the days of ancient Greece. Then, when the fulness of the time was come, the mind of God came down to meet the mind of man, and Jesus was born in the East. If the mystic pyramids speak of the sunrise glory of the Orient, and if the Parthenon symbolizes its culture, then the little grotto of Bethlehem represents the last and greatest gift that has come from the East to bless us. Out of the East cometh light. We of the West are proud and glad in the sunshine. Let us not forget gratitude for the mysterious and bountiful Orient, which has been the ultimate source of all the brightness that has come to bless our world.*

* " Four Princes," Scherer, " Foreword."
NOTE.—In his thoughtful book on " The Problems of the Far East," Mr. G. Curzon summarizes

JAPAN TO-DAY

But now, is it not strange that the great continent which has so blessed the world the vast importance of Asia after the following manner:

It has been the cradle of our race, the birthplace of our language, the hearthstone of our religion, the fountain-head of the best of our ideas. It has supplied a scene for the principal events, and a stage for the most prominent characters in history. Of Asian parentage is that force which, more than any other, influenced, transformed, and glorified mankind,—namely, the belief in a single Deity. The six greatest moral leaders of the world were born of Asian parentage and lived on Asian soil: Abraham, Moses, Buddha, Confucius, Mencius, and Mohammed. The Lord Himself chose Asia for His birthplace. The most famous and the wisest of kings have sat upon Asian thrones. Alexander and Napoleon turned thither as towards the only theatre befitting their enormous ambitions; the latter with the amusing, petulant exclamation, " This old Europe tires me!" The three most populous existing empires are Asian empires. From that mighty land of the sunrise has come the noblest product of all literature, in the Old Testament of the Hebrew Scriptures. Thither proceeded the embryos of modern science in the empiricism of Arabian geometers and metaphysicians; and it was there that the mariner's compass first guided men over the trackless waters. On Asiatic soil were

GATES OF ASIA

should itself be at this time without the blessing of the light? Palestine, the outward opening gate, is neighbor to Persia and Arabia; yet Persia and Arabia are not Christian countries. Palestine, the outward opening gate, belongs to the same continent with India and China; yet India and China are to-day two of the greatest fields for missionary activity. It is but a step from Palestine across the Isthmus of Suez into the great continent of Africa; yet Africa is known as the Dark Continent. But remember that the light, coming out of the east, shines always straight towards the west. How glorious is the east at the time of the sunrise! and yet it is the glory of sacrifice, of self-emptying;

reared the most astonishing of all cities, Babylon; the most princely of palaces, Persepolis; the stateliest of temples, Angko Wat; the loveliest of tombs, the Taj Mahal. There, too, may be found the loveliest of nature's productions, the loftiest mountains on the surface of the globe, the most renowned of rivers, cataracts which make Niagara seem pygmy, and the most entrancing of landscapes. In the heart of Asia lies to this day the one mystery which the nineteenth century has left for the twentieth to explore,—namely, the Thibetan oracle of Lhasa.

JAPAN TO-DAY

it is the sacrificial glory of birth. Look at the east an hour later, when the sun is hurrying like a busy man towards his western home,—how leaden and gray and barren the east seems then! But, as surely as light travels in an orbit, so surely will the sweet blessed sunshine, having made its worldwide circuit for the giving of light and life,—so surely will the sunshine come back into the east from the other side, and the east will be uplit again.

From Palestine the Gospel spread towards the west. In almost a straight line it journeyed, through the Cilician gates, to Ephesus, Corinth, and Rome. So gentle, so quiet was its diffusion that few guessed its strength until, in the year 324, the whole Roman empire became Christian by imperial decree. By the commencement of the seventh century we find the light so spread as to cover every land in its western track, to the very outermost edges of Gaul and Spain, while the whole northern fringe of Africa, lying in the line of light, is ablaze with Christian churches. Moreover, from the outlying edges of Spain and Gaul the rays had been refracted northward to Wales and Ireland, among the Scots and Picts.

GATES OF ASIA

During the next two centuries the Germans and English are converted; in the tenth and eleventh centuries Scandinavia is added to the Christian map, which now includes almost the whole of Europe. And we know that when those Europeans sailed across the Western sea, the light came with them, ever broadening from that single star which appeared in the East to the shepherds of Palestine, so that to-day the entire sweep of Europe and this farthest Western world is in its blessed pathway. Out of the East came light.*

And the light returns to the East, through the West. If Palestine is the gate opening outward, Japan seems the gate opening inward. When the Church had been quickened into activity by the virile touch of the West, we find this activity manifesting itself by the desire to have the light of the Gospel, now that it had traversed the globe, reach Asia from the other side. Accordingly, the Roman Church, energized by the tremendous potencies of the German Reformation, sent Xavier to India. But he, as Paul to Macedonia, was divinely called over into

* " Four Princes," p. 260.

JAPAN TO-DAY

Japan, where "a great door and effectual" was opened unto him. He and his successors, as we have seen, met with remarkable favor. It was a time of growth scarcely equalled since the Apostles. But, as with the early Church, so now persecutions came. It was finally thought that Christianity had been exterminated. For three hundred years Japan was a hermit nation. Then, in 1854, the country was opened once more, and missionaries soon came in. From that time to this the progress has been steady and sure, until to-day mission stations are to be found in every province of the empire.

What is more, Christianity now wields an influence out of all proportion to its mere numerical strength. For it has made remarkable headway among official classes, so that active Christian men are to a large extent directing the destinies of Japan To-Day. One member of the Imperial Cabinet, two speakers of the Lower House, and two justices of the Supreme Court, with scores of minor officials, have been zealous members of the Christian Church. Out of three hundred members in the first assembled Parliament, the president and eleven constituents were Christians; this was fully nine

GATES OF ASIA

times as great a representation as the relative strength in the population would admit. The most recent reports inform us that " in the present Parliament the president and thirteen members are Christians. Although the opposition to Christians is strong, yet members are elected even from the strongholds of Buddhism. The army records show one hundred and fifty-five Christian officers, or about three per cent. of the total corps, and the two best battleships are commanded by Christians. Especially in literary and educational circles Christians are a leading power. The native preacher, Kozaki Hiromichi, declares that scarcely a single book has been published during the rule of the present Emperor that does not show the influence of Christian thought. At the universities and other higher grades of schools Christian teachers and pupils are very largely represented, and the public life and thought of Japan is being gradually saturated with Christian thought and expressions."

But the chief significance of Japan lies in this: Japan is the inward opening gate of Asia, the John Baptist to China and her neighbors. On Japan's western side lies that

JAPAN TO-DAY

mighty continent of Asia, the now darkened source of all the world's light; the earliest home of man, the birthplace of civilization, the field for the development of the Old Testament Church, and the birthplace, finally, of Him who is the Light of the World. Almost within arm's reach, across the Yellow Sea, is China, now like some huge carcase under the clutches of the eagles of Europe. If proximity means anything, if racial kinship stands for aught, if centuries of the same literature and the same civilization have had any influence, Japan, with ready receptiveness for new truth, is the natural saviour of China, the intermediator between West and East. The very qualities that differentiate these peoples from each other make it feasible for the doughty lad to rouse the sleeping giant. They were at war a few years ago; and yet that blow which Japan struck at China was simply a blow of awakening. The slumbering giant first rubbed his eyes when this impulsive little David went forth with the smooth pebble of civilization in his sling. Unless China makes the mistake which Goliath made, and persists in laughing at the lad with his pebble, a civilized and Christian Japan may be

GATES OF ASIA

the chief instrument under God for the civilization and Christianization of China and of Asia. We cannot doubt that among Japanese Christians may arise some alert and zealous Paul, who, with Luke and Barnabas, Silas, Timothy, and Titus, will at length press into the heart of Asia with the cry, "Arise, shine, for thy light is come!"

The problem of China to-day is vexing the whole wide world. As one has said: "Its combination of horror and remoteness and mystery makes a powerful appeal to the imagination. It is as though something that had appeared to be a huge, inert, misshapen, lifeless mass had suddenly revealed itself as in reality a frightful monster, thrusting its head a little way out of the impenetrable gloom, wherein one hears, although one cannot see, the writhing of its hideous coils." It is not without significance that the symbol of that mighty empire is the dragon. The Baron de Constant, an international authority on world politics, declares that "we are only at the beginning of the Chinese peril; it transcends our imagination." The gist of the danger lies in the fact that this enormous mass, inert for centuries, has

JAPAN TO-DAY

at last begun to move. What its future track will be none can foretell. One thing is certain. China and the world from this day forth can never be as they have been. Along the dawn of the twentieth century lies a great, threatening cloud, which may, however, have a silver lining. But the cloud is there. The problem confronts us. A few years ago the sacred capital was actually invaded, the inviolable rulers were forced to flee, and all those mighty masses, hitherto unmoved, have since been in one continual ferment. As our former consul at Tien Tsin said, the doom of the ancient *régime* has been sealed, for its continuance depended, as it were, upon the seclusion within the holy of holies, from the profane gaze of mortals, of the so-called Son of Heaven. China has moved. And Napoleon, at St. Helena, looking out on the vast empire of the world, which he had come to know so well, said: "When China is moved it will change the face of the globe."

Consider the vastness of the mighty empire, comprising four millions of square miles and four hundred millions of souls. That is to say, the country is one-third larger than Europe, and the people comprise a

GATES OF ASIA

third of the population of the globe. But these figures are too nearly an approach to infinitude for the finite mind to grasp. To be impressed with the mere bigness of China you must go there. One traveller has graphically described the experiences of all: You are dropped down in China. Immediately the people swarm about you. They seem to rush in upon you through every pore. You see and hear and breathe nothing but Chinese. The whole four hundred millions of these beings seem to weigh you down and crush you. Then by and by it dawns upon you, with sometimes overwhelming force, that you have not merely entered among a countless mass of strange human beings, but that you are face to face with an alien civilization—ancient, complex, mysterious. Wonder grows to amazement, curiosity to awe, when you learn that this is in many respects the most remarkable civilization the world has known. Its antiquity seems like that of the eternal hills. We know that it extends as far back as two thousand three hundred years before Christ. But the actual beginnings are lost in the darkness of early Arcadian and Egyptian days. This empire saw the empires of the ancient world blaze

JAPAN TO-DAY

up in all their brief brilliancy—Babylonia, Assyria, Persia, Greece, Rome, Israel. It saw them die out and pass into oblivion, but it went its way unchanged. It was known to the ancients of the West, but always as a vague, hazy, mysterious country. The Greeks and Romans write of its people under the name of the Seres. Ptolemy, 300 B.C., speaks of them as the Sinæ. And it seems probable, on the authority of great Biblical scholars, including Gesenius, that Isaiah referred to them 700 B.C., when he predicted that "these from the land of Sinim" shall come to worship at the throne of the Messiah.

One of the chief sources of the perpetuity of this race is its marvellous degree of physical vitality, and this in spite of an almost total disregard of the commonest laws of health. Instances without number might be cited to illustrate their wonderful vitality. One must suffice, as indicative of great vital power coupled with extreme longevity. When the provincial examinations were held a few years ago for promotion in a sort of system of civil service, one governor reported that nine candidates over eighty years of age and two over ninety went through the pre-

GATES OF ASIA

scribed test, and sent in essays of which the composition was good and the handwriting firm and distinct. But another governor reported that in his province thirty-five of the competitors were over eighty years of age and eighteen over ninety. These records are accurate. Could any other country afford a like spectacle? It has truthfully been said that if people with such physical endowments as the Chinese possess were to be preserved from the effects of war, famines, pestilence, and opium, and if they were to pay some attention to the laws of physiology and hygiene, there is reason to think that they alone would be adequate to occupy the principal part of the planet and more.

The incident just cited serves to indicate another source of strength with the Chinese: their great intellectual power. Confucius is one of the great names of the world, and so is the name of Mencius. Chinese literature is said to be profoundly interesting. Their modern diplomatists are sometimes more than a match for our own. We date the beginnings of modern science from the three great mediæval inventions of printing and gunpowder and the mariner's compass. But these were not, properly speaking, inven-

JAPAN TO-DAY

tions at all, but mere discoveries, since they had been known in China for many centuries. Movable types were first used in Europe in the fifteenth century; they had been used in China a thousand years before our era began. Gunpowder had been known there for hundreds of years before it was introduced into Europe. As for the compass, we find the first mention of its use in Europe during the twelfth century, but it is thought to have been known to the Chinese for twenty-four centuries at least.

Physical and intellectual strength, however, will not make a nation great without deeper qualities of character. There must be industry, frugality, perseverance. Now, there cannot be the slightest doubt that in these three great basal qualities of character the Chinese are greatly our superiors. Their diligence is untiring, their patience a marvel, inexhaustible; while their simple mode of life is a rebuke to our growing habits of self-indulgence. This is the unanimous testimony of all who have lived in China.

Nor are they lacking in honesty, or in benevolence, or in filial piety. Whereas in essential respects they are of a most degraded morality, they nevertheless have

GATES OF ASIA

learned an important lesson which the Japanese have as yet signally failed to learn; that "honesty is the best policy." Commercial residents of the Far East, British or American, will assure you that they would rather do business with Chinese than with their own countrymen, because, on the whole, they can better trust them. Their filial piety is known the world over.

Finally, in summing up the elements which make the Chinese problem of such profound significance to the Western world, it should be remembered that the Chinese, next to the Anglo-Saxon race, are the greatest colonizers in the world. "The large islands and coasts of Malasia are being occupied by them. They are flocking into Polynesia and America. Hardy, thrifty, persevering, able to endure any climate in the world, they are to be the great agents for redeeming such lands as Borneo, Sumatra, and other tropical regions, where the white man sickens and the natives only vegetate, until pushed out by the enterprising Chinese."

We now have before us the chief factors which constitute the vast potential strength of this mighty empire. I say "potential,"

JAPAN TO-DAY

for China is still a sleeping giant. China invented the compass, but is without a commerce; discovered gunpowder, but is without arms; invented movable types, but is without a press. Their best mode of locomotion has been the wheelbarrow, and in consequence they have suffered frequent and devastating famines in a land of plenty. They have in a single province coal-fields sufficient to supply the world for twenty centuries, but are without mines, because disturbances of the ground might, forsooth, disturb the dragons. "They are embodied conservatism. For twenty centuries they have lived in a state of arrested development, well satisfied so to live." True enough. But the present crisis, as was said just now, lies in the fact that this period of stagnation seems about to end. China has begun to move, albeit in her sleep. In 1894 Japan gave the first rude shock to this ancient slumberer, and events are surely completing the awakening. I ask, what is to happen to the world when this slumberous giant shall have been fully aroused? At present all that the Chinese need is coherence. Their troops are not lacking in bravery; they have proved many times that they have reckless daring

Japan at War
From a drawing by a native artist

GATES OF ASIA

almost without parallel. All they need is leadership. What if some Napoleon or Jenghiz Khan arise among them? Remember the vast population: a third of the entire population of the globe. Remember these great qualities of physical vitality, intellectual strength, industry, frugality, perseverance, commercial integrity, and instinct for colonization,—which is another name for conquest; imagine these people united by some one common interest, under a great leader, and animated by an intense hatred of the Anglo-Saxon race, which they will not hesitate to manifest by savage cruelty, and you will see what the world might have to face.

I believe this to have been an animating idea with Europe of late years in its attitude towards China, as well as a desire to acquire new territory. With nations, as with individuals, "self-preservation is the first law of nature," and the statesmen of the West have seen that "the yellow peril" is more than a myth and have now and then endeavored to secure dismemberment as a preventive against great future dangers. Russia especially has favored such a policy. Nor would any grave question of rights be involved. Those people are mistaken who inveigh

JAPAN TO-DAY

against the partitioning of China on ethical grounds, because it would not be just to deprive the people of self-government. For, as a matter of fact, the Chinese are already ruled by aliens, and have been since the thirteenth century, when Jenghiz Khan, the Tatar chief, conquered the country. The present rulers of China are not Chinese, but Manchus. The distinctive head-dress of Chinese men, the queue, was in its origin a badge of subjection, being ordered by one of the conquerors in sign of his mastery. Therefore the dismemberment of China would not be its disfranchisement, but simply transfer from one form of vassalage to another, and perhaps far better. The question, then, is not one of right, but of expediency.

But it has come to be the general opinion, outside of Russia, that such a policy would by no means be expedient, on account of the inevitable jealousies of the powers. China would become a source of continual contention. The question of the Far East would be permanently added to the Eastern question and to all the other questions which perplex the world's mind to-day. The great states would be compelled to augment in-

GATES OF ASIA

definitely their armies and fleets, already ruinous, while they kept continually on their guard one against another. "At this sight," says Baron de Constant, "the countries of disorder and fanaticism, the Mussulmans of Europe, Africa, and Asia, will grow bold and will begin again with impunity their persecutions against the commerce and the persons of Christians."

The fact is, China must have simply a guardian,—to direct and protect as an elder brother guards a wayward overgrown child, until China shall be changed from within. Another fact is, that the contest for the guardianship of China is in progress at this very moment. It is a great wrestling match between Slav and Saxon, between Russia on the one hand and the Anglo-Saxon peoples on the other, as represented, paradoxically enough, by Japan. It is not in the least altruistic. The nations are not vieing for the elevated privilege of averting the "yellow peril" from their neighbors at cost and self-sacrifice to themselves. To be the custodian of China means to hold the key to the future. It means the possession of strength and of wealth untold. The power that dominates China will hold the balance of power for the

JAPAN TO-DAY

world. As regards natural resources, the immense country is a veritable Golconda, only waiting to pour its boundless wealth into the lap of the most favored nation. It possesses the richest mineral deposits in the world, as yet altogether untouched. Its markets offer the most tempting outlets for surplus products. Its internal commerce promises unlimited possibilities of development. And then, there are always the people,—one-third of the whole human race! What an alliance to win their friendship and secure their co-operation for purposes defensive and offensive! Plainly, the custodianship of China will practically mean to become the custodian of the destinies of the world.

Russia has never lost sight of this fact. While the other nations of Europe have wondered and pondered over the problem of China, Russia has stealthily, but steadily, strengthened her grip upon China. She has never receded, she has always advanced. With an astuteness that puts much other diplomacy to shame, she has let the other nations work her will. She let Japan fight China ten years ago and win a brilliant victory; but, when the little catspaw had thrust itself into the fire and pulled out the ripe

GATES OF ASIA

chestnut of "Manchuria," the Bear quietly put his own great paw down over it, and Japan was forced to submit. Russia then hastened to build the Manchurian railway, in the guise of the saviour of China; but, as Senator Beveridge has said, "the plain result of the Manchurian road is that the only business route to China is through the dominions, under the protection and surrounded by the influence of the Czar." Russia was very meek during the war that resulted from the Boxer uprising; only insisting on self-protection by sending her troops to the borderland of Manchuria, and promising soon to withdraw them. But she has made her hold there stronger every day. Fully a year ago, at the very time when Russia had bound herself to evacuate, we were told that the military officers were bringing even their wives and children to the stations, "and the building of permanent barracks goes on without relaxation." Mr. J. Sloat Fassett now informs us that Russia has spent more on the development of Manchuria than England spent on the whole Boer war.

It must always be remembered that the Russians, like the Chinese, are essentially

JAPAN TO-DAY

Oriental. It was only three hundred years ago that they began to have any intercourse with Western Europe; and their intercourse has since been marked by a steady career of conquest. They are even Oriental in their spiritual sympathies. The so-called Christianity of Russia is a religion very different from our own. It is not without significance that it is known as the "Eastern" Church. Very early in the Christian era did this breach begin to appear between the churches of the East and the West—a division which inhered in the nature of things. Upon these diverging faiths as a basis, divergent civilizations have been reared; so that Russia, building upon a religion that was Oriental in its origin, has remained Oriental to the end. As Mr. A. Maurice Low expresses it, "The Russian is at heart an Oriental veneered by Western civilization, with a natural leaning towards his origin. It is easier, far easier, for the Russian to revert to his original type and become an Oriental than it is for him to be in sympathy with Western nations." And "many scientific observers believe that if Russia is given unrestricted sway and permitted to become the hegemon of Asia, in the course of time the Asiatic will be ab-

GATES OF ASIA

sorbed into the Russian and a new mixed race will be the resulting product." If that day shall ever come, the Anglo-Saxon race will straightway make its exit, and Napoleon's prophecy of Russia's universal dominion will be fulfilled. The issue, therefore, is clearly joined. Russia's aims towards China are positive and aggressive. The aim of the Anglo-Saxon nations is rather negative and defensive,—not so much the possession of Chinese custodianship for themselves as to keep it away from Russia, on the principle of self-preservation. It is a great and fateful game that the nations to-day are playing on the chess-board of the world.

Russia has colossal astuteness, but the fault of the colossal is that it despises the little. Russia's supreme mistake has been that she has despised and underrated Japan. Her attitude towards this little empire has, until very recently, been that of contemptuous condescension. And this makes precisely the smart that Japan can never forget or forgive. The Japanese hatred for this huge enemy is bitter beyond all belief. And the scheme of opposition has meant the quiet ingratiation of herself with China, that Russia's unblushing courtship might be secretly foiled. There are signs that Japan has not failed. For example, Japan has become the Chinese educational Mecca. "It is the fashion nowadays," said the *North China Herald* last spring, " for Chinese of all ranks and professions to go to Japan if they want to learn anything." There were then fifteen hundred Chinese students in the various schools of Japan, including two hundred non-commissioned officers undergoing military training in Tōkyō. On the other hand, the Chinese have been entirely unwilling to go for their education to Russia. "Add to this the fact that Japanese is now the official language in the Peking University, that the Chinese government is going to engage a Japanese adviser on International Law, that Japanese educators are being introduced throughout the whole country, that Japanese scholars have been engaged for the compilation of a new code of laws,—and you have strong indications that if war were to take place between Russia and Japan, China's sympathies would be with the latter," wrote a deep student of the East a month or two ago. And have not her ablest statesmen now begun to intimate the fulfilment of this

GATES OF ASIA

prophecy, in their most recent press dispatches? It is my own most steadfast conviction that Japan has the secret sympathy of China, and that Great Britain and the United States would be well advised in favoring an alliance with her as against Russia; for China is to be reached, I believe, best through the mediation of Japan, and therefore it is no mere figure of speech to call this little empire the gate of Asia.

But, when China has been reached, what is to be done with China? What measures can be taken that will ensure a harmonious relationship with the West? This question is answered when we ask what it is that constitutes the common bond of the people of the Occident, and find that it is the tie of religion. It is not pertinent to object at this point that the religion of the nations is an inconsistent and even hypocritical profession. That may conceivably be true. But this does not affect the undoubted fact that religion, and religion alone, apart from remote ethnical ties, is the one common bond that links America and England and Germany, and even France and Italy and Spain, into a certain unity of thought and action to

JAPAN TO-DAY

which the people of the Orient are alien. You cannot otherwise classify Western lands than as so-called "Christian" nations, whose tie is the "Western" Church. Religion is the only adequate brotherhood, the universal equalizer of ideals and conduct. In all ages it has had more power over the minds of men than any other single influence. During the passage of years it must inevitably mold the national as well as the individual character. And so if China is to be brought into an identity of spirit with the West, so that she may live on terms of intelligent peace with the nations of the West, the transformation must proceed from within; the same spiritual influence must be applied to her that has been applied to these. There, if you please, is what might be called the political argument for missions.

And, again, I insist that the key to China need only be large enough to fit the small door of Japan. Japan, not Russia, is the gate from the West into Asia. Close racial kinship with China has stood Japan in good stead. It must needs be a strong bond, indeed, that leads a huge nation to seek the instruction of a pygmy that has just chastised her; but China seeks the tutelage of Japan.

GATES OF ASIA

And, strangely enough, the tutelage of Japan is "Western." The Mongolian of Japan has stronger Western sympathies than the Slav of Russia. These sympathies extend even to his religion. The "Eastern" Church of the Slav has had scant success in Japan, as compared with the churches of the West. Russia has built her great cathedral on a commanding hill in the capital, and sent out the great missionary, Nicolai, who in strength has been second only to Verbeck; but Japan has turned from the magnificent "Eastern" cathedral to the quiet little chapels of the West, and Nicolai has scarcely possessed a fraction of the power and prestige of Verbeck. Christianity, whether it come from Russia or America, is still in its origin and essence Oriental; but in the latter case it has gone forth in its natural orbit, and returns into Asia enriched by the treasures of the lands it has touched in its circuit. Japan has stretched forth her hand for our civilization, and the form of religion she chooses ought naturally to be that whereon her chosen civilization has been founded. The signs of the times plainly indicate that such is to be the case.

JAPAN TO-DAY

So will the cycle of history be completed. So is missionary work in Japan invested with intense human interest. Japan is the gate to Asia. And as the light shone out from Palestine two thousand years ago, so now we see this other gate swing inward, that the orbit of the Sun of Righteousness may be complete. "He walketh in the circuit of the heavens." "For as the lightning cometh out of the east, and shineth even unto the west, so also shall the coming of the Son of Man be."

Now that the bloody seeds of war have actually been sown, what shall the harvest be? That is the question uppermost in every thoughtful mind. No man can answer it. One shudders at the possibilities of the question. Suppose that Germany, with her strenuous "war-lord," with her sympathies quickened in behalf of her noble and majestic kinswoman, the beautiful, sad Czarina; with her interests stirred for her large Shantung possessions in China, and with an erroneous, but natural, interpretation of the so-called "yellow peril,"—suppose that Germany concludes to "make a diversion in behalf of Russia that shall have world-wide

GATES OF ASIA

consequences," as has already been intimated from Berlin? Or suppose that the excitable French, misled by their dubious alliance with the Czar, should throw themselves into a quixotic leap-to-arms against the little yellow soldiers of the East? Or suppose that England, whose naval forces are already in a state of alert, but quiet, preparedness, who is jealous of Russian encroachments against India, and who has recently entangled herself afresh in the Far Eastern situation by her strange expedition against Thibet,—suppose that England, whose nominal alliance Japan secured several years ago as an offset to the Russo-French alliance, should commit some overt act that would make this union with Japan not only nominal, but actual? Or, suppose the most imminent danger of all, that Russia, frantic to cover the shame of a feared defeat at the hands of a small Asiatic power with the smoke of a larger war, shall succeed by hook or by crook in seducing some other nation to work her terrible will—what then? From such disaster may the "God of Battles" save this war-cursed world. The fire which now burns in the East would spread as quickly all throughout the West as when the red rising sun suddenly shoots above the east-

JAPAN TO-DAY

ern horizon and kindles the whole world into flame! But if the neutral nations shall continue to exercise that remarkable and noble self-restraint that they have manifested during the past few years, under circumstances almost as trying as these are, and shall leave Japan and Russia to "fight it out," with Korea as the ostensible bone of contention, but with the huge booty of China as the secret ultimate prize,—what then shall be the result?

I am neither a prophet nor the son of a prophet, but I am nevertheless led to believe that if Russia and Japan are left unmolested in this war, the neutral nations only seeing that they give fair play, then the chances are, perhaps, with the pygmy as against the giant. Why? Chiefly for the following reasons:

1. Japan is ready, whereas Russia is unprepared for war. In the year 1894, when Japan concluded her war with China, and Russia, backed by France and Germany, coolly proceeded to deprive her of her booty (that very peninsula which is now the chief arena of the struggle, with Port Arthur as its key), I was in the educational employ of the Imperial Japanese Government. As such, it became my duty to be present at the

GATES OF ASIA

various meetings held in Saga to celebrate the victory over China. Every address had the same key-note: Revenge. *"La Revanche"* does not mean one-hundredth part as much to the patriotic Frenchman, thinking of Alsace and Lorraine, as "Revenge" has meant during the last ten years to every Japanese, who has thought all the time of Liaotung and Port Arthur. And they have steadily prepared to make their revenge a reality. Every cent of the enormous Chinese indemnity went immediately to the strengthening of an already competent navy, and to this sum millions of dollars have been added by the political champions of an aggressive naval armament, on which point all Japanese legislators, however divided concerning other questions, have invariably been as one man. Russia, on the other hand, has sneered. As I said just now, the mistake of the colossal is to despise the little, as David was despised by Goliath. Russian officers have told their soldiers that the Japanese are "a race of monkeys," who cannot fight. And I have conversed frequently with Russian diplomatists familiar with the situation in the East. When I would ask them what they thought of Japan

JAPAN TO-DAY

as an enemy, the reply has always been, in substance, the typical answer which I received from the strongest Russian diplomat whom I have known. With his little finger he flicked the ash from the tip of his big cigar, and said: "*That* is what we think of Japan." Consequently, Russia · was not ready. She never really expected that war would come. Alexieff, and even the peaceful Czar, complained with an almost ludicrous pathos, on the 10th of February, that the Japanese came at them before they were ready. If it be true of coin that "he gives twice who gives quickly," it is still more true of blows. And Japan is not only prepared with quick offensive measures, but she has also been swift and thorough to defend. I know from personal examination somewhat of the thorough defences of the entire coastline of Japan. The Russian fleet has complained that snow-storms have kept them from shelling Hakodate. I suspect that the snow which they feared was the upward fiery snow of thickly-planted submarine mines.

2. The brilliant initial victories of Japan will tend to impair the foreign credit of Russia. Dr. Albert Shaw, one of the best informed men in America on the foreign situa-

GATES OF ASIA

tion, wrote in his journal a few weeks before the war opened that if Japan could only force the fighting on Russia, and gain a succession of swift, brilliant victories on the sea, Russia would be terribly hampered, because her sinews of war would be cut,—namely, her reliance on foreign loans. But, he added, Japan will scarcely be able to force the fighting, for the Russian ships are shut up in impregnable harbors, where she will quietly keep them, while Japan fumes and frets outside. Japan, however, entered the impregnable harbors, and accomplished the feat which Dr. Shaw declared would cut the Russian sinews of war.

3. Japan is fighting near at home, while Russia will be hampered in maintaining connection between her various and difficult bases of supply. The Japanese know every foot of the waters they are fighting in, and are also thoroughly familiar with the land. For many months they have had spies, disguised as Chinese coolies, and speaking the Chinese dialects, working along the line of the Siberian Railway. Already bridges have been cut, and there will surely be more to follow. It is equally easy to embarrass the Russian attempt to maintain connection

JAPAN TO-DAY

between the naval bases of supply. Japan, on the other hand, has her stores and repair shops at her elbow. When a Japanese admiral is embarrassed, he just trips over to Sasebo, and, after breakfasting, so to speak, like Dewey, he is ready for the war again.

4. For these and for other reasons the resources of Japan are far more easily convertible, and far more quickly mobilized, than those of Russia. Russia is unwieldy; Japan is agile and alert. Russia is embarrassed by her very bigness. And, while having more than fifty times the territory of Japan, she has only thrice her population. Russia has been like some misguided farmer, who, instead of cultivating the home farm, has spent all his substance always for more land, more land. Russia is diffuse, undeveloped, crude. Japan is concentrated energy.

5. Japan is upheld by national support, Russia is hindered by a national apathy. Japan did not need to make a foreign loan at the outset. Her request for a hundred million dollars, was quickly covered four times over by her own people, coolies vieing with capitalists in their contributions. But newspaper correspondents in Russia have reported absolutely

no responsiveness on the part of the people to this war, until very recently, when there is strong reason to suspect that "the enthusiasm of the masses" has been manufactured. We foreigners have come to think of the enthusiasm of the Russian commoner, when he has any, as an enthusiasm for bombs to be used at home.

6. The patriotism of the Japanese, on the other hand, is a frenzy, a passion, a religion, a fanatical abandonment and absorption of his whole being in his country's cause. It is impossible to exaggerate the intenseness of Japanese patriotism. It is taught from babyhood as the quintessence of morality, and it is practised as the highest virtue of manhood. Japan, during all of her history, has never been successfully invaded; and I fear that should this ever be done, no victory could be achieved short of complete extermination, just as when Titus invaded Jerusalem. Indeed, the only perfect parallel in history for the extreme nationalism of the Japanese is offered by the Jewish nationalists against whom Titus fought.

7. Finally, this war is, with Japan, a sheer struggle for existence, whereas it is with Russia a mere struggle for more territory.

JAPAN TO-DAY

Ever since the bear put down his heavy paw upon the Liaotung Peninsula and withheld it from its owner he has been pushing stealthily forward against this despised, but presumptuous, little foe. Not until the wisest of the Japanese statesmen perceived that Korea would meet the fate of Liaotung did they yield to the national desire for war. For they were fully alive to the serious issues involved in a war with Russia, and were extremely anxious to avoid it if they could. But they knew that the integrity of Korea is absolutely essential to Japan's existence. "Korea in Russian hands means a dagger pointed at the heart of Japan." Moreover, the Russian encroachments in Korea were but a step, as they perceived, in Russia's constant advance,—in line with a consistent endeavor to hem the Island Empire in on every side, until finally the bear might crush out the very life of the little nation with one mighty, comprehensive embrace. If ever in history a nation has been driven to bay, that is the case with Japan. But she had been expecting it, and was prepared for it with a thoroughness that has astonished the world. The world was surprised when Japan conquered China. And, notwith-

GATES OF ASIA

standing the immense power of Russia, I think it is not without the bounds of possibility that the world shall be surprised still further, in view of all of the considerations that have just been named.

If Japan conquer, what then? Paradoxical as it may seem, I persist in believing that this will mean the salvation of China, the triumph of the West in the East, the supremacy of Saxon over Slav, and of Christianity over paganism. War is terrible. But when it comes, then it behooves us to study conditions carefully, and bestow our sympathy where it is deserved. The Japanese are by no means an ideal people. One dreads in particular to contemplate their overweening conceit in case of the defeat of Russia! But in this case Japan has right upon her side, and, besides, she is building far more widely and more deeply than she knows. The foundations of this war touch the very vitals of the world; it has consequences of profound importance for you and me. For the solidarity of the race is a fact accomplished. What is done in the East affects us here in the West. The Russo-Japanese war is a world-problem. Who shall hold the key to the Orient?